C000088599

RUNNING THROUGH WHEATFIELDS

David Singleton

Grosvenor House
Publishing Limited

This book is published by
Grosvenor House Publishing Ltd
Link House
140 The Broadway, Tolworth, Surrey, KT6 7HT.
www.grosvenorhousepublishing.co.uk

A CIP record for this book
is available from the British Library

This book is a work of fiction. Any resemblance to
people or events, past or present, is purely coincidental.

ISBN 978-1-83975-286-5

Introduction

For Michael Megson

I wrote this memory of my childhood almost ten years ago, mainly for my family, who I thought might have some interest in the soil in which I was born. Actually, they had precious little, and so I forgot about this bit of autobiography until a couple of years ago, when I was made more acutely interested in my childhood by the resumption, after more than 50 years, of contact with my childhood friend Mickey Megson.

Neither of us now lives anywhere near the Black Country: Mickey lives in Bury St.Edmonds, and I live in Lancashire, on the edge of the West Pennine moors. Neither of us regrets moving away, but we have walked the scenes of our childhood escapades together: two old men in uncertain health, completely anonymous in places where once we were known to many. Mickey's memory of our boyhood is more vivid than mine, and he has reminded me of the many dirty tricks in which we were partners. In a real sense, this is as much his book as mine, and it is dedicated to him.

All memoirs of childhood are records of loss, and so is this. Mickey and I were part of the post-war generation that were given unprecedented opportunities for upward social mobility. We both benefited from them, to a modest extent; we could now, should we choose to do so, describe ourselves as "middle class." I have, largely without meaning to, acquired the manner and accent associated with the social status to which I now pretend; Mickey has been less concerned to do so, perhaps truer to himself.

I do not regret this, but there is a corresponding loss. There is now nowhere that I automatically think of as home – if by "home" one means the place where one feels no necessity to act a part, being certain of acceptance for what one is. There is now, for me, no such place: nowhere where I feel sure of automatic acceptance. This book describes what was, for me, home, and the process by which I began to be selected out of it, by way of an education that has equipped me with a style that would have appeared alarmingly alien in the Wednesfield in which I grew up. It is a process millions went through, and it is only interesting up to a certain point. My adolescence and early manhood were an age of frustration, anxiety, occasional success, frequent humiliation. As such, they are almost completely uninteresting, even, in retrospect, to me. I have therefore stopped this memoir at the point where my life lost the familiar glamour of being securely at home.

Contents

Where we were

St. Thomas' Church, Wednesfield

It is reasonably certain, not that it is a matter for scholarly debate, that I was born and lived my early life in the Black Country. One can never be quite sure, because the term "Black Country" is not a precise geographical expression. It is certainly part of the West Midlands, and it certainly does not include Birmingham, as its inhabitants will argue with pained expressions. Whether Wolverhampton is part of the Black Country is a matter of personal taste, though hardly fierce controversy; it is not an area that evokes strong emotions, positive or negative.

There is a minor mystery over the place of my birth, though again it is not a matter of fierce learned controversy, or even of great interest to me. I think I remember, as some people do, the actual moment of my birth: it was cold, excessively bright and came as an unwelcome intrusion. However, I was not within sight of a sign identifying the place in which I found myself, and my mother was somewhat vague subsequently, showing herself in this to be a true

Black Country woman. My passport says I was born in Sedgley, but my birth certificate places the nursing home in Lower Gornal. The Gornals! The name suggests an obscure venereal disease, rather than a place, but if I was born there, I can only say that it was not my fault. I was not consulted in the matter. The decision, like so many, was made by my mother. She was entitled, she believed, to give birth in a nursing home, because,

"Yer Dad was in the RAF,"

And the Rosemary Ednam nursing home offered a higher standard of comfort than was commonly available in that epic winter of 1947.

There is no mystery about where we lived: it was in Wednesfield, which is now indistinguishable from Wolverhampton, but was then separated from it by extensive wastes of slag, accumulated over about a century of industry. Children growing up today know the evocative word "slag" purely as an expression of opprobrium for ladies of easy virtue. There were such ladies around, even in the nineteen-fifties, but we called them "old bags," or, alternatively, "ooers," then. "Slag" was the constituent element of what in those days passed for our green belt: elderly heaps of spoil, grown green with the years, with pools of collected rainwater filling abandoned mineshafts. This was what, for the first dozen or so years of my life, represented for me "the countryside." The spoil heaps were my mountains, the pools my lakes, the canals my winding rivers.

The main such area we referred to as "Bacca's End," I have no idea why. The existence, nearby, of a certain "Backhouse Lane" perhaps suggests an explanation, but it is not one of which I can be certain. In the summer, I played cowboys and Indians., usually with my mate Mickey, on the spoil-heaps and fished for tadpoles in the pools. In the winter, we walked on the creaking ice that – occasionally – spread over the standing pools. We have recently rediscovered winter in England; we knew it well enough then. It was dark, prolonged and cold.

There was one slope, more recent than the rest and exceptionally steep, down which we slid on rusty corrugated iron sheets, invariably ending in a giggling heap. Our mothers did not of course know that we were doing this, though they must have guessed. After all, they had themselves benefited from precisely the same amenities when they were children. But it was not then the fashion to be over-scrupulous about the care of children, boys or girls. In school holidays, we were turned out of home after meals and set a time before which our presence was not required.

Wednesfield, as was true of much of the Black Country in those years just after the war, was not greatly changed from what it must have been in the mid-nineteenth century: the main public buildings were still there: the pubs, the working-men's institute, where people went to pay their "club", to save for Christmas or, in macabre fashion, to bury themselves, the Methodist chapel, the Sunday Schools, the park, the church. The cemetery was about half a mile away, at the end of a muddy lane, which the Council has now, I see, egregiously chosen to call "Memory Lane." It had no name then. Many of the nineteenth century terraces were still there, some with sties still attached, though I knew no one who actually kept a pig, much to my regret. The predominant impression was one of scruffy improvisation: the area had never quite managed to tidy itself up from the first industrial revolution. It had been too busy, and so at that stage it remained. There was the great factory: the Weldless Steel Tube, at the bottom of my grandparents' street, out of which men on bicycles poured at the end of the day in crowds that Brueghel would have delighted to paint, thousands upon thousands. A mile away, across the border in Willenhall, was the Yale lock factory. Willenhall still manufactures ninety percent of the world's locks (and presumably therefore also keys), according to the Black Country museum, a statistic that may make you swell with pride, or blanch with scepticism at its obvious improbability.

The identifying product of Wednesfield was not at that time as repugnant to all respectable feeling as it has subsequently become.

This was animal traps, designed to accommodate any creature, from a mouse to a lion. Not that lion-traps were an immediate need in the Black Country, but they became more relevant when exported to, say, Bulawayo. Growing squeamishness about the plight of furry creatures trapped in the iron jaws of a trap has written finis to the pain and terror my home town was once pleased to export around the globe, particularly those extensive regions of it that had the great good fortune to be coloured red in the pages of the atlas.

Almost all of this has now gone. Bacca's End is no longer an unconvincing effort at a Lake District: it is mostly covered by a retail park, called, for no obvious reason, Bentley Bridge, and a faint effort has been made to gentrify the "cut". Most of the terraces were replaced by jerry-built semis in the 70's or by tower blocks a little earlier. Both of these are now showing their age in a way their sturdy predecessors did not. The pubs are struggling: there is now "Franky and Benny" and "Fatty Arbuckle" to attract a different clientele: more affluent and certainly more obese. Though "affluent" is no longer a word readily to associate with the Black Country. In the 50's, it epitomized a country which found itself instructed by its millionaire Etonian Prime Minister that it had "never had it so good." No one was rich, but there was work for all who wanted it, and everyone did. Margaret Thatcher put an end to that. "Unemployment," we were sternly told, "was a price worth paying." For what, we never did quite discern. It did not appear to be a sentiment which consoled the Lady herself when a cabal of grateful colleagues presented her with her P45.

When I was a boy, Wednesfield was grimy, busy and useful. Now, it is less grimy, not particularly busy and, so far as I can tell on the few occasions I return, usually to meet my childhood friend, predominantly retired. It looks weary, as though its vital force has somehow expired. There always was a slight air of world-weariness about Black Country people, expressed in a humour that is gentle, self-deprecating and doom-laden. The two quintes-sential Black Country characters were a duo of labourers called

Aynuck (English: Enoch) and Ayli (Eli); they were celebrated in the local paper, in printed collections of stories and finally in a comedy duo that did the rounds of local working-men's clubs for some years. A typical story has Aynuck going into a library and asking if it has a book on fool-proof methods of suicide. The female librarian replies:

"Ar, but I ay givin' it yo'. Yo woe bring it back."

Gerrit? Not perhaps uproariously funny, but characteristic in its assumption that suicidal despair is both usual and funny, and in its representation of women as a source of disapproving authority.

What I recall first about Wednesfield was the omnipresent odour of soot: soot from the coal which everyone burned, from the barges on the canal carrying coal from the still extant coalmines (Thatcher saw to that, too), soot in the smoke that issued from the factory chimneys and the funnels of steam trains, soot in the clothes people wore or that hung on the washing-lines each Monday. For my first dozen years, I probably assumed that oxygen itself tasted of soot.

For the first few years after the unwarranted intrusion of my birth, my parents and I lived at my grandparents' house in Hart Road. The road still exists, but has been turned into a cul-de-sac, suitably traffic-calmed; when I was a boy, there was no traffic except the crowds of cyclists emerging from the Weldless Steel Tube factory at the bottom of the road, and they were calm enough, after a tenhour shift. My dad worked there; so did two of my uncles. My granddad had done so briefly, during the war.

My granddad had previously been a miner. He was the third of four brothers called, in a staggeringly impressive piece of family planning, Matthew, Mark, Luke and John. How this was achieved, I can hardly begin to guess, but I used to feel that the third gospeller had drawn the short straw. Since then, Luke has once more become somewhat improbably fashionable . Luke Thornsbury he was, born

5

of a line of manual labourers. My cousin has traced our family back, as people often do when they approach old age, and found nothing of significance, except that her own mother was conceived, though not born, out of wedlock. The Thornsburies have left, from generations of backbreaking labour, no obvious impact on the world, being all of that class which is born to be forgotten. My granddad left school at eleven, and went to work, until he reached the age of 65, which occurred three years before I was born. I was the first grandson, and this gave me a special éclat in his eyes.

"That lad'll have letters after his name,"

He would say from time to time, somewhat improbably.

Many of my first memories are of him. He was one of those men on whom a hard life has the same effect as that of kneading fingers on modelling clay. It had made him soft and pliable. He was not ashamed to cuddle his grandchildren when they were little, just as he had given his own children such mothering as they received – for his wife, my grandmother, was a remote, uncommunicative woman with little capacity for affection. I knew him of course only in his extreme old age, when he still had some of his miner's strength and squareness of build. When I was old enough, he would take me out with him, pulling me on the cart on which he transported the bundles of kindling wood he sold to augment his old-age pension. He had his round of regular customers, and was as popular with their animals as with them. He always had a bag of fishes' heads for the cats and a biscuit for the dogs. He had been for much of his life politically active, latterly as a Socialist, originally as a Lloyd George liberal. A photograph of the Welsh Wizard adorned the parlour, beside the aspidistra. I was not allowed in there, which gave it some of the quality of a shrine.

There were two rooms and a scullery downstairs in our house. The scullery was stone flagged, and had only cold water running from the only tap in the house. In winter, it frequently stopped running. It was as though the freezing point of water was especially high in Wednesfield. A brief cold snap in November – compulsory in those years of more predictable weather cycles – would leave us without water until the feeble heat of candles set beneath the pipes could coax out a few drops of liquid once more. January would bring a more prolonged drought.

The world was colder then. I remember the piercing cold of that scullery, and the rapidity with which the bathwater, poured from kettles into a tin bath, would become at first lukewarm and finally cold, with a repulsive, greasy scum on the surface. I remember the way ice would form on the inside of bedroom windows, so that you could write rude words in it for your mother to discover. I remember the way we crowded around the fire, our faces reddened, our backs freezing, postponing as long as the bladder would permit, the moment when you had to leave the fire and go outside to what we called the "lar-pom."

There were six of us in the house: my parents and I, my grandparents and my uncle Luke. I do not know whether my grandfather ever aspired to foster a quartet of evangelists, as his own parents had done. If so, his ambitions had been swiftly dashed. Against family tradition, his first child had been a girl, my Aunt Florrie, born in 1904, too close to my grandparents' wedding to be wholly respectable. Perhaps in response to her unorthodox conception, of all my family Florrie was the one with strongest aspirations to propriety. She lived five minutes' walk away in a semi-detached house: something that seemed to me in my early years to be both luxurious and exotic. Houses came attached to each other in terraces, backing onto terraces, with tunnels called "entries" about every third house, and tiny gardens, each with an air-raid shelter designed to offer protection on the assumption that the Luftwaffe might exhaust their supply of bombs and drop melons or cricket-balls instead, for they could have kept out nothing more substantial.

All my granddad's children lived within shouting distance. Approximately 200 yards away, Florrie was the most distant.

Harry and his wife Betty lived at the end of the same terrace, sharing their house with Harold and my Aunt Hazel. We lived with my grandparents, and Luke lived with us too. He cannot have been much more than 40 then, but my Uncle Luke seemed to me the most ancient being I had ever seen: grey and shrivelled like Tithonus. He spent most of every day, when not in the garden, crouched on a piece of furniture that might, in a different sort of household have been called a chaise longue. To us, it was just the "settee" and Luke had the end of it next to the fire over which he would crouch with smoke-blackened toast, and often with bacon congealing on a tin plate set on the black-leaded grate. He seemed, curiously for one who was cadaverously thin, always to be eating, nibbling like a giant rat. He had, I was told, once been to work, but it did not agree with him. It was understood that Luke suffered from his nerves, perhaps proportionately to his capacity to get on other people's. He had possibly inherited a family tendency to depression; he may even have been schizophrenic; certainly, he was possessed by a lethargy I have often had to recognize in myself.

Having "nerves", he had also, as was to be expected, artistic talents, or at least propensities: my mother once said to me, in awe:

"Luke went to art school, you know."

I doubt this. I cannot see how he would have fitted it in. I think he may once have done a correspondence course; if so, he subsequently ignored it. Certainly though, he had a desire to create and a degree of primitive skill. My mother had, I think, a painting of his, which hung for years in my parents' sitting room. It is a naïve Black Country idyll: a bridge over a canal, with a small boy and a girl fishing as a bargee leads a shire horse away from them along a road that appears to emerge from the water and to end in a cloud. Almost everything is wrong: the shadows are at right angles to the apparent source of light – a large object like a yellow Brussels sprout that one takes to be the sun – and the perspective is inebriated. But there is a quietness about it that lets you see what the artist wanted you to feel. No one now knows what in the end happened to this painting. A pity: I should like to have it, though not to display it.

Luke's chef d'oeuvre, however, was his garden, which was a kind of paradise in miniature: formally laid out, with tiny beds and box hedges and pedestals carved from wood, on which perched doves of every colour, also carved from wood. Wild birds were not encouraged, and the pedestals were surrounded by boards studded with sharp, upward-pointing nails to discourage the local cats from approaching. At the centre of the garden was a small, white aviary, made by Luke, in which flew canaries, lovebirds and java-finches. This eccentric, but strangely compelling, miniature Stourhead was much admired, of necessity from afar, since Luke allowed no one other than my grandparents to enter, and them strictly observed. Nor did he seek to disseminate his creativity. My Aunt Florrie once asked him to carve her a dove.

"I'll watch ah doe,"

Was his conclusive and graceless reply.

That is how we lived then: in close proximity. To add to the six humans, there was also a dog: a spaniel called Peter, whom I remember attempting to ride. The stink of humanity – of chamberpots, household washing, breath, unwashed flesh – of cooking and the pervading reek of the coal fire must have been overwhelming, but I remember it mainly as comforting, and along with the omnipresent closeness of other beings went a curious Puritanism. It was never possible to forget that Man was a corporeal being with gross bodily functions, but reference to those functions was strictly taboo. It is assumed today that working-class people behave in their homes like the Royle family. That would not, I think, have done for my grandmother, who was as fastidious as the Queen Mother herself, perhaps more so. I guess the lack of privacy and absence of adequate washing facilities must have done something to reduce whatever fleshly desires there might otherwise have been. Otherwise, there being little chance of adequate contraception, people would have bred as fast as microbes.

There were, to my recollection, few books in the house, but there was a radio, or as we called it then a wireless, on which we listened to Family Favourites and, later and curiously, Round the Horne. I have often wondered what my parents and grandparents made of Kenneth Williams, or of the repartee of Rodney and Charles . They knew, of course, that there were men whom they called "cissies", marked by their dislike of football or of such essential manly pursuits as catching artillery shells in their front teeth, but I think it would not have occurred to any of them to wonder about the sexual proclivities of such beings. Whenever, on Family Favourites, a record by Kathleen Ferrier was played, which was frequently, a reverent hush would descend, and my granddad would wipe away a tear:

"Ar, that wench cor arf sing,"

He would opine knowledgeably. I have never subsequently been able to dissociate that most joyous of singers from a sudden ecclesiastical hush on a Sunday morning, with the cabbage over-boiling in the scullery next door. Quite unfairly, her voice automatically provokes in me that faint discomfort, that slight sense of personal inadequacy ,one associates with things "churchy." My granddad loved equally the tenor John McCormack, recently dead, whose records he played repeatedly, displaying a distressing liking for the decidedly schmaltzy. Thus, we had repeatedly, Macushlah, her sweet voice pleading "that death is a dream and that love is for ay." Some hope, on both counts.

These then were the physical circumstances in which we lived, my family and millions like us in the years just after the war: the years first of Mr.Attlee, then of the returning titan, Winston Churchill, the years of rationing and of a stammering but well-intentioned monarch, soon to be succeeded by his daughter. It was an austere life, perhaps even an impoverished one, though for the most part we did not experience it as such. We did not much feel the lack of money, there being little in the shops to buy with it – we did not in any case venture much beyond Mr. Waddington's one-room shop across the street. And we knew no one who was significantly richer. We knew vaguely that there were people "out on the Cannock road" who lived in what we called, in awed whispers "private housing," but we did not know them, and they were not in a hurry to know us. Had it not been for the atmospheric concentration of coal dust, we would have been reasonably healthy, living as we did on a diet largely prescribed by the gentleman in Whitehall.

I do not remember very much of the three or four years we lived with my grandparents: vague impressions, rather than concrete events, have remained with me. I recall my fear of falling down the earth closet and being swept away, and I remember picking up a bright red sweet, only to discover that it was the glowing end of a cigarette. That should have taught me a lesson about the capacity of life to disappoint. I fear it did not.

Cold

Do you remember when we were young
How cold it was? At night, the fire
Left a memory of itself in the blackened
Grate, and the ice drew silhouettes
Of mountains behind the drawn curtain:
Yellow ice in the frozen chamberpot,
And the lavatory outside across the yard,
Water solid in the tank. We shat
Less often then, before bathrooms
Invited us to linger. Like a faithful dog,
The cold was always there, inside
And out, bringing urgency to movement
And sharpening the pointed stars.

My Family

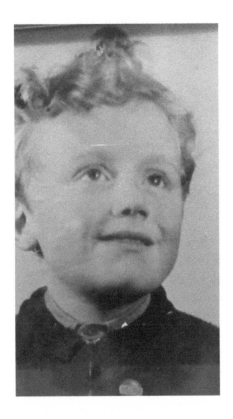

The author at six. The badge, belying his true nature, says "helper."

It was clear from very early on that my dad was not like other men; at least, not like the other men I knew. Curiously, people remember him as tall, which he was not: he was at least two inches short of six feet, though he became powerfully built, through a combination of hard manual work and beer. He had about him a sort of presence that probably derived from a consciousness of being a bit cleverer than most of those around him. Unusually, he was not a local man. He was born and lived his early life, till the age of seventeen, in what was then still firmly Cumberland, occasionally Cumberland-Westmoreland, but most certainly not "Cumbria." He spoke occasionally of Cumberland as a kind of lost Paradise – but made singularly little attempt to return there. His family had been farmers – tenants and labourers, not landowners – for generations somewhere west of Pillar, and in his childhood he had walked miles to school in all weathers, "across the fell." He had passed the examination to go to the local grammar school, but his mother had been unable to afford the uniform – a common enough story in that generation; so common, in fact, that actual failure in the examination must have been comparatively rare. Nevertheless, I think he always saw himself as a scholar manqué, and felt himself to that extent slightly superior. Certainly, he could be, especially when drinking, effortlessly patronising.

He had also served in the armed forces, as a regular, not a con-script, during the war, being in this respect unique among my immediate acquaintance. My granddad and uncles, other than the one who was rumoured to have deliberately sawn off his trigger finger, had all been in reserved occupations, their contribution to the war being restricted to the Home Guard and the Fire Service. My father had been in the Royal Air force, as ground crew. Not that that had been without its dangers. He spoke little about it, but one of his jobs had been to fly with pilots testing new planes, listening to the engine for possible faults. It was standard practice to turn the plane into a steep dive, and briefly turn off the engine, to see if it would subsequently come on again. If it didn't, you could find yourself distributed over much of Eastern Scotland. My Dad had been stationed in Aberdeen, and claimed to have seen the Northern Lights. Later on, he had been seconded to the Eighth Army in North Africa and Italy, where his mechanical expertise had been directed to the maintenance of trucks. He had received a mention in despatches for carrying out a repair under fire, as my mother told me after his death. It had not counted against him that he had stolen the spare parts from the next truck in the convoy. My mother also once told me a macabre tale about his killing an Alsatian that attacked him when he was on guard duty.

Even the wildest imagination could not have attributed to my dad anything of a romantic aura. He was too sour, too awkward, too plain in appearance for that, but his exploits at least gave him the kudos of someone who had been a little further than West Bromwich, who had seen foreign countries, and taken real chances. This was enough to make him unusual in my family.

He was also strikingly more competent than any of my grandfather's sons. He could fix any machine you put in front of him, if you gave him long enough, from a lorry or an aeroplane to a lady's watch. Much of his time outside work was spent repairing neighbour's clocks, which he did partly for the love of it, and partly to be able to demonstrate an amused contempt for the feckless owners, who allowed themselves to be defeated by such essentially simple entities as springs, levers and cogwheels. No one taught him this. He had simply an eye for how things worked, and for what needed to be done to them when they failed to work. He could do the "Times" crossword; he could read and enjoy A Hemingway novel; and he could jump over a five-bar gate from a standing start. He was not a loquacious man, and his very taciturnity, coupled with his frequently acid tone when he did speak, helped to give him a formidable air. He was, it was generally agreed, an "awkward bugger", but he attracted a grudging and universal respect.

Dad had entered the RAF to escape the limitations of life in West Cumberland, but if this spoke of ambition it was one that he failed singularly to pursue. For all his abilities, he rose no higher than foreman at the Weldless Steel Tube, in charge of the gas producing plant, with perhaps 12 men working to him. He never owned a house, never paid more than a hundred pounds for a car, and in all his life took only one foreign holiday: to a concrete hell-hole called

15

Lloret de Mar. In middle age he changed career, and became, for a while, a pub landlord. In this, he was in the end unsuccessful, because the role of landlord's "missus" was uncongenial to my mother, entailing as it did regular, serious work. This was not the only ambition she was responsible for frustrating. At one time, he hit upon the idea of buying what was essentially a slum house, doing it up, and then moving in. He would have had both the skills and the energy to do that, but Mum put her foot down. She was much impressed by the rather pleasant council house Hazel had just moved into, following a period in which she had decamped to the West Country in protest at cohabitation with relatives.

I often wonder how much it irked him that to outward appearances he achieved so little in his life. Certainly, as he grew older, he often appeared discontented. It was not that he was a lazy man. Far from it, he worked seven days a week, until lunchtimes on Saturday and Sunday, and such spare time as he had he for the most part spent working around the house, or on one of our succession of cars, purchased for around £50. Nevertheless, he had seventeen years tending to the gas producer, beside the canal, his nostrils filled with the scent of boiling tar, and it was not until quite late in his forties that he attempted to move on.

Then, the attempt, though in the end futile, was at least thorough-going. When I was 17, and had a place at University, my parents, without discussion with their teenaged children, applied for emigration to Australia. I am not quite sure what they thought I would have done in Australia, but I suspect that my educational future, and my sister's, was not prominent in their calculations. We filled in forms, and trooped off to Birmingham for medicals, and for some months it seemed inevitable that we would go. It cost £10 in those days. My parents were, however, quite close to the age limits, and it was discovered that my father had seriously high blood pressure. He was turned down, a failure that he found humiliating. A year or two later, he became a pub landlord, a change of profession that he treated as an opportunity to work further on his hypertension, turning it from serious into terminal.

Why he was so timid for so long. I don't know, but I suspect that there was, underneath the appearance of superior competence, a basic lethargy or timidity that disabled him, made him shrink from anything resembling a risk. In this respect, my mother was the least suitable possible partner for him, deeply fixed as she was in attitudes confirmed by the depression and by a history of barely getting by. To any proposal that smacked of ambition she would always, throughout her life, exclaim:

"Yo've got big ideas, yo 'ave!"

It was her most devastatingly contemptuous dismissal. I don't know whether, or how often, my father entertained "big ideas," but they would not have found a receptive audience in my mother.

I was not of course aware of this in my early years, when it no more occurred to me than to any child that my parents had limitations. I suspect that my first few years of life were extremely happy. I was my granddad's pet, and my father, unusually for that era, enjoyed looking after small children, and made up for any lack of competence in this regard my mother might have displayed.

My sister arrived when I was about two and a half. I remember her being fetched back from the hospital, a small white bundle with blue ribbons.

"This," I was told, "is your sister."

I can't say that I was especially elated or even interested in what seemed to me a rather tedious, in fact barely animate, object. At first, I entertained some hope that she might be returned to the hospital, but swiftly reconciled myself to the dismal fact that we were now a family of four, to which was added a black and white cat: a graceless, semi-feral creature, whom it was dangerous to approach.

My dad, however, liked the fact that he was a father of two small, helpless creatures: he bathed and changed us, read to us, sat us on his knee, and generally did all the things that fathers do these days, but are supposed not to have done when child-rearing was women's work. I wish I remembered those years better, for I suspect he displayed a tenderness then that I do not recall him displaying as we grew older and became competitors, rather than dependents.

My mum was a Black Country woman to her core. She spoke with the accent of the area, and with its characteristic imprecision. All her life, she had difficulty in recalling names, or indeed nouns of any kind. She once breathlessly reported an accident in the words:

"Mrs Whatsit's got a whatsit stuck up her whatsit and she's been taken in a whatsit to the wheresit."

The information content of her conversation was, then, perhaps not unduly rich, but to compensate there was a great deal of it. She was voluble, excitable, quick to anger and to remorse, deeply sentimental, limitlessly affectionate and charmingly egotistical. She was the youngest of five children, and very much the baby, and pretty enough to attract a flattering amount of attention. None of her brothers was capable of the degree of focus implied in suggesting that they "doted" on her, but she was at least much humoured, and my granddad made up for any deficiencies in mothering my grandmother may have been guilty of.

Not that her life had been easy. None of their lives were easy, living in a small terraced house, born during the great flu epidemic after the First World War, enduring the Depression and then Hitler's War. Coventry was only thirty miles away, and the industrial Midlands were a prime target throughout the war. My mother had worked in a munitions factory, and had become outraged at the conditions in which the girls worked. Consequently, she brought them out on strike, not necessarily a prudent move in conditions of total war. She was hauled before a magistrate, who fortunately took the view that the grievances expressed were amply justified.

However, this was not uncharacteristic of Mum's approach to work. For it to be palatable, it had to be undemanding, lucrative and carried out in perfect conditions, preferably by someone else. I never knew her to work for much more than a month at a time. She had, I believe, been the only member of the family at work at one point in the thirties. From then on, she rather assumed that she had done her bit, and settled down to be served for much of the rest of her life. My father earned enough to maintain us all and to keep himself in beer, and my mother trained my sister and myself to become an unpaid delivery service, so that she need leave the house, only when she wished to, in order to go "canting" with one of her friends, always to the accompaniment of several cups of highly sugared Camp coffee. Bottles of Camp coffee were one of the defining objects of my childhood, with their Imperialistic motif of a kilted soldier being served by a deferential Indian. Their contents, being mainly chicory, had little in common with coffee as it is usually conceived, but it was good enough for my mother and her pals. Mother – in common with her friends – was much given to repeating the adage that "a woman's work is never done", but the reasonable interpretation of this was that it was rarely actually commenced. There was, of course, housework to be done, after a fashion, but it left plenty of time for leisure.

My dad once remarked to my mother:

"Everybody likes you. It makes me sick."

It was true. Everyone liked Sarah, and her popularity was wholly disproportionate to any effort she made. She was above all a great teller of stories, and would shake with mischievous laughter as she recounted some mishap – like the tale, often told, of when my Aunt Hazel, who was immensely fat, tucked her dress into her knickers by mistake and walked down the road thus attired. My Mum of course did not at the time bring this eccentricity to her notice, for that would have spoiled the fun. She frequently spoke of her childhood. If a tenth of what she had to say can be believed, the children of her era were almost incredibly lawless, wandering around in large gangs permanently engaged in behaviour that today would attract the notice of the bench and impair the digestion of right-wing Tory MPs. She told tales of gang warfare, of ruthless victimization of the vulnerable (children who were "simple" or "not all there" or "puddled", of whom there were uncomfortably many, were ruthlessly mocked) and of organized theft from enraged but powerless shopkeepers . Not that her memory was unfailingly exact; she recalled a Wednesfield that was a sort of Arcadia, with fields of rolling wheat, pools and copses. Actually, it could not have been anything like that for at least a century and a half.

My mother was born in 1919 and therefore educated in those years between the wars which are now frequently referred to as a Golden Age of intellectual rigour, when children were made to learn "the basics" in an atmosphere of absolute discipline. This seems to have been entirely fanciful. My mother could certainly read and write, and do simple arithmetic, but no effort seems to have been made to engage her intellectually (though admittedly the effort would need to have been Herculean) in any subject whatever. She spoke, frequently, of a schooling of which the characteristic tone was one of enmity between teachers and pupils. The latter did as little as they could get away with, and the former kept order through regular and arbitrary caning, sarcasm and public humiliation. It was, for example, a rule that the "dunces" sat at the front of the class, so as to be confronted on an hourly basis with a failure that, though actually attributable to the mockery of an education they were given, was firmly ascribed to their own inadequacy. My mother was given three strokes of the ruler for the following exchange:

"Who knows what we call an inhabitant of Paris? Sarah Thornsbury, your hand is up?"

"Please Miss, a Parisite."

Cue for laughter, as on a later occasion:

"What is the capital of England? Don't any of you dunces know? Yes, Sarah?"

"Please Miss, London."

"Be quiet, you morons, she's right."

Mum told these stories without affection certainly, but also without resentment. Education was not to be regarded as a public benefit, still less as a pleasure. It was a kind of prolonged childhood disease. Something, like mumps and chickenpox, that happened to you, but which you got over without any lasting effect.

My parents met in 1940 because my father was stationed nearby in Cosford as part of his service in the RAF. He was by no means one of the Few; rather he was one of the many with time on his hands because at that point the War had not really got going. I do not know where they met, but I believe it was on a blind date arranged by someone else. People of their generation did not talk to their children about what they would have been bemused to hear described as their "relationship." After all, it was none of their business and, whether pleasure or pain, it had to be got through, like the rest of life. Long after my father's death, I took Mum to the Black Country Museum, where she was mildly interested to see the bridge over the canal, since it had been taken there from Wolverhampton, and was familiar from their courtship. Often, my parents would linger on that bridge for the last few minutes before my father caught hs train. Then, Mum would say plaintively, "I 'ad ter walk whum," an inconceivable distance to her, but in fact not much more than a mile and a half. Whatever happened on that bridge will have been decorous and certainly confined to above the waist, because that was largely how things were then. There is a rumour that sexual morality became somewhat less rigorous during the war, but if this was true elsewhere, it was not true in Wednesfield.

My sister believes that my parents' marriage was physically very intense. I have no idea, beyond a general male suspicion about how women talk, how she knows this, but there must have been something that kept them together. Generally, they were about as compatible as matter and antimatter. My mother was excitable, talkative, affectionate and quick to anger; my father was taciturn, remote, often sarcastic and conscientiously awkward. He was also a drinker: not, quite, a drunkard, but a steady, conscientious bender of the right elbow, especially at the weekends. He was not one of those made jovial by drink. Instead, he would become patronising and argumentative, pointing out any deficiencies of which he had been made aware in the household or its members. Since the household depended largely on my mother's talent for housekeeping, this was not difficult to do. Mum would invariably respond with fierce indignation to any criticism, however justified:

"You do the bloody washing, then."

Or

"You do the shopping."

As I moved into my teens, there would be shouting-matches, and occasionally physical violence, most weekends. I feared that this would culminate in separation or divorce, from the age when I began to understand that such things could occur.

Sometimes, I have read that couples decide to separate "for the sake of the children." My whole experience tells me that this is complete self-delusion or deliberate dishonesty. Each Saturday night, I would lie in bed sleepless, waiting for my father to come home, with a feeling of acute nausea in my stomach, as though I had swallowed alive some small but sharp-toothed animal. I would catch the quality of his voice as he entered the house; often, there was a particular shade of bonhomie that meant that he was intent on provoking trouble. Often, too, no provocation was required, since my mother too was spoiling for a fight. Words would be exchanged, then shouts, sometimes blows, and I would wait, crucified by anxiety, for it to stop, and for my parents to go to bed. Through it all, year after year, my greatest fear was that it would stop for ever: that my father or my mother would simply leave. So, they acted out their dissatisfaction with each other and with their lives, to my misery, and my sister's, but I am still grateful that they stayed, however painfully, together. I was also grateful, if mildly surprised, that when my father died, my mother's comment was:

"Well, we 'ad forty good years."

And, even more improbably,

"E never looked at anyone else."

Once my father broke off from one of their rows, and burst into my bedroom (we moved away from my grandparents' house when I was three or four).

"'Ave you been up the top cupboard?" He shouted.

This was the top shelf of a cupboard in the living-room. It could be reached only by climbing, and it was understood, though I do not recall any specific prohibition, to be out of bounds.

"No. It wasn't me."

In fact I had. My father kept a pair of military binoculars, by which I was fascinated, there. I had clambered up to look through them, and had then replaced them, carefully as I thought.

"Don't tell me yer bloody lies."

With that, he turned me over and proceeded to smack, very hard. His hands were not especially large, but they were teak-hard from manual labour, and he was a strong man. Again and again the right hand descended, as I sobbed and scream. At one point my mother half opened the door and sobbed:

"Oh Al, doe 'it 'im."

His response was to push the door shut on her and continue. At some point I wet myself in fear that my dad would actually kill me, so violent did the beating become. At last he stopped, and I lay there, sobbing and soaking wet. Then, I have no idea why, he charged in once more and began again, smacking hard on both buttocks and legs with the flat of his heavy hand, hitting now against already bruised flesh. The terror and bewilderment were worse than the pain. I never knew what made him so angry.

Hours later, it may have been the following morning, my mother came in, lifted the bedclothes and screamed:

"Oh look at 'is bloody legs, Al."

As she wept, my father entered the room and went white as he saw my bruised legs, red and purple from the beating. He sought to embrace me, but I moved painfully away. Weeks later, I entered the showers – I was in my first year at Grammar School – and a boy called out:

"Look at Singo's arse. It's all bruised."

My backside instantly became the focus of an interest it has seldom evoked subsequently. A teacher was fetched, and I underwent a deeply humiliating interrogation as I constructed somewhat transparent lies to conceal what I suspected might have become a difficult event for my father. It has always seemed paradoxical to me that my main emotion was one of shame that I should have been treated in this way, but I know that other children have reacted similarly. Fortunately, as I thought, the school took it no further, and the incident was not repeated. My parents continued to smack us, but there was never again such a paroxysm of self-indulgent violence. I cannot imagine what resentments, what envy, what self-hatred, what consciousness of insufficiency went into that degrading night.

But I was older then, and close to adolescence. When we left my grandparents' house I was still barely more than a toddler. I remember the move. I remember being set on a bare, wooden table as our few bits of furniture were moved into what seemed a space of vast and echoing emptiness. The house, still rented, to which we moved was a three-up. two-down at the end of a small terrace, but the rooms were large and high, whereas those I had been used to were small and low-ceilinged. It was probably about 60 years old, built in the late nineteenth century when in the Black Country it was common for houses to be cheek by jowl with small factories and workshops. There was a disused factory next to the backyard, used by our neighbour, a dour Boer War veteran called Mr.Munday, as a workshop, and a working factory (called simply "The Factory") next door. We shared a lengthy drive with Mr. and Mrs.Munday, and we had an L-shaped backyard, which never quite became a garden, in spite of occasional sporadic and unconvincing efforts by my father. Originally separate from the house, but joined to it by a wooden verandah, constructed around a drain that could become fragrant in summer, if by some meteorological freak such a phenomenon as summer actually occurred, was a large scullery, with a well and a cold-water tap – the only one in the house. Next to the scullery was a coalhouse, and next to that the lavatory. There was of course no bathroom and the only heating in the house was from the fire in the living room. The pipes were of lead, and froze in the winter. These somewhat impromptu arrangements did not cause us any dissatisfaction. That was how people lived. It was how my grandparents lived. Change of habitation brought about no change in life-style, if such a notion had been invented.

Our neighbours, Mr and Mrs Munday, played a significant part in our lives. Mr. Munday was, as I have said, rumoured to have fought in The Boer War. He may, while fighting, have been infected with the Boer outlook on life. He was silent, sour and immensely diligent. His garden, like my Uncle Luke's, was an eccentric paradise, at the end of which he had constructed a summerhouse made from wood primarily reclaimed from used orange-boxes. It was possible to clamber from our garden onto the corrugated iron roof of this frail edifice, and I often did so, miraculously escaping both capture and injury. Mrs Munday was quite unlike her husband, no doubt benefiting from her lack of contact with native Afrikaans speakers. She had a grown-up daughter, Muriel, who was married to Thomas, but no grandchildren, and it was clear that she liked the company of small children. She was a reliable source of sweets and biscuits, not just to us, but to our corgi, when he arrived. He would march around and scratch at her verandah door. When asked what he wanted, his eyes would turn greedily to the biscuit-tin. Duly rewarded, he would then immediately depart, demonstrating precisely the same level of social grace as his two young owners.

Both the Mundays were well over seventy when we first knew them, and both died, in the proper sequence: husband first, then after a decorous interval, wife. We were still quite young, and they may well have been the first people who disappeared from our lives. I do not recall grieving, precisely, but I do remember feeling that a gap had appeared in my daily existence: no more comforting presence next door.

I have mentioned that I had a sister. I will concede that her existence was never more than a minor inconvenience, for the most part barely noticed. She was a generally quiet little soul, much given to reading and, when old enough, playing complicated and uninteresting games with other little girls. She was, however, when quite small, inclined to sporadic and surprising acts of violence, for which I was usually blamed. I recall that once, when she must have been two, she was given a new pair of what appeared to be diver's boots, but were referred to by the inappropriate diminutive "bootees". She tottered about as I played on the carpet, fully absorbed in a new Dinky toy. For the purposes, presumably, of testing the hitting power of the said "bootees", she crept over to me, drew back her right foot and let me have a pile-driver flush on the point of the nose. I let out a wail of agony and indignation, whereupon my mother rushed over:

"What's up with yer? If yo've banged yerself, yo've only got yerself to blame."

Thus, I learned a valuable lesson: that the concept of evidence as applied between male and female was somewhat elastic. Female innocence was taken for granted, whereas male guilt was assumed, whatever the evidence.

I recall an example of this from when I was about 12. My friend Ian and I were sitting in his house, blamelessly discussing how to spend a day off school. His Mum came in from shopping, and clouted us both soundly around the ears.

"Wot's that fer, Mum?" he yapped.

"There's a lad in the street blartin'. I knowed yo and that bugger'd 'ave summat to do wi' it."

Convicted with neither trial nor evidence, precisely as Messrs Blair and Straw intended for terrorists. Of course, we had tripped the unfortunate lad, as he made the cardinal error of sprinting joyously past us. But that was not the point! The point was that there was no evidence to that effect. We smarted at this injustice, unconsoled at the reflection that we got away with far more crimes than we were punished for.

So, I learned early the male lesson that nothing is ever a sister's fault. That apart, though, I do not remember our doing very much together, at least voluntarily. We were often taken shopping by my mother, there being nothing else to be done with us, and occasionally told to sit and be quiet while my mother "canted " or "rattled" to her female friends. We were not expected to participate in these

27

conversations, and adults would have found incomprehensible the idea that children had a right to be entertained. We were repeatedly told that "little children should be seen and not heard" and that we should "speak when spoken to." This latter was usually in response to fatuous accusations, such as:

"Oo, 'e ay arf growed, ay 'e?"

A question I assume was rhetorical, and which always provoked a smile of pleasure from my mother, who may have been in some indirect way responsible. Or:

"Ay 'e got lovely 'air, Sarah?"

"Ar," my Mum would reply, "'e takes after 'is dad."

This was utterly incomprehensible, since my father had been largely bald from quite an early age; clearly my mother meant that I resembled the descriptions she had heard of my father as a child.

This snatch of conversation illustrated one of my Mum's many eccentricities. She never referred to her husband by his name, which was Alan. It was always "'is dad" or "'er dad," or, if she was speaking directly to one of us: "yerdad." Even after I married, when she was discussing her husband with her daughter in law, Mum would refer to him, perhaps somewhat confusingly, as "yerdad." In effect, it became his name.

I think that my sister was affected more obviously by the contentious nature of my parents' marriage than I was. She became somewhat lethargic, but also very studious. Both of us read voraciously, but she was much more inclined than I was to read what she was supposed to read. She did very much better than I did at school, until she was about 15, when she suddenly lost interest altogether, left school at 16 and within months became involved with and subsequently married at the age of 18 to, a far from suitable man, by whom she had two children and whom she eventually divorced on grounds of cruelty about ten years later. Her life has never fully recovered from this cataclysm, from which my parents did nothing effective to rescue her.

My father's family was far away in the Lake District, but my mother's friends and relatives were all around us. She never went to the shops (known collectively as "The Village") without encountering one or more. The ensuing conversations would always begin with the formulaic greeting:

"Am yer better?"

It seemed always to be assumed that Wednesfield was perpetually in the grip of some epidemic, of universal application. Invariably, conversation centred upon the maladies suffered, it appeared, by all the adults with whom my mother was acquainted, and there were a great many of those. In those days, despite the great upheaval of the war, Wednesfield was a very settled community. That minority of men who had been to war mostly returned, if they could, and there seemed no good reason subsequently to move away. Work, skilled and unskilled, was plentiful, and if the Black Country had no great intrinsic attraction, that was true of any area in the country where work was to be had. Thus, my mother for much of her life was surrounded by people with whom she had been to school and among whom she had grown up. It was common to refer to people, like characters in an epic poem, by a brief genealogy:

"Yer know, Iris:' er wot married Mr. Whatsit's daughter. Im with the club foot."

Or

"Sid – 'im wot lived down by the cut. 'E 'ad a brother wot was killed in Burma."

Incredibly, these less than specific descriptions always prompted instant recognition, or a pretence thereof. It was a town in which everyone knew, not only everyone else, but everyone else's business. Inevitably, in such a closed society, people found themselves attributed "characters" which it was hard for them to dispel. A woman, for example, might have been rumoured to have had a fling with a soldier during the war, and would remain forever "an old bag" or "no better than she should be." Another might pronounce her aitches, not necessarily in the orthodox places, and be known as "stuck up." A man might be known, on the basis of a single altercation, as argumentative, or "awkward."

Everyone knew someone, like my uncle Luke, who suffered from "nerves" and such people were tolerated and, to a degree, looked after, though little or no attempt was made to diagnose, still less treat, whatever emotional or neurasthenic condition was at the root of their suffering. A few unfortunates were committed. It was said that they had gone "to Stafford" and the threat that one would end up in Stafford was used to quell such childish eccentricities as being too engrossed in books. One or two others lived a marginal existence as tramps. " Old Herbert" was one such. Heroically filthy, he lived in a shack made of sheets of corrugated iron underneath a railway bridge on the fringes of Bacca's End. The combination of vile smell and his reputation for devouring children prevented us from approaching too closely, but my friend Mickey and I considered it great entertainment to rain chippings down from the railway line on to the sides of his hovel. He would then emerge, waving his fist and emitting a string of obscenities that we thought something of a triumph to have elicited. This was an era when swearing in front of children or women was still frowned upon, but Albert was so generally frowned upon that he gave little heed to this particular source of disapproval .

My mother's nearest sibling, both in age and in geography, was my uncle Harry, who lived at the far end of the same terrace. He was a small, humorous man, who was never to be seen without bicycle clips. Unusually, he did not drink, but he smoked Woodbines continuously, lighting the next cigarette from the embers of the one about to be extinguished. He had been a considerable footballer in his youth, and retained a spectator's interest in sport. He was animated by the conviction, for which there was some evidence, that the recent history of English sport , was one of inexorable decline. This was especially true of English cricket, with particular reference to Colin Cowdrey, whose occasional failures he would greet with sardonic relish and whose regular successes he would acclaim as temporary aberrations:

"Caaardrey!" he would sneer. "Fat bugger! 'E's useless. Got eighty? Bowlin' must've been pretty ropey."

"Bowlers," he would cry, for he was of the Geoffrey Boycott school of cricket commentary, "I've shot 'em. They couldn't get a bloody blind school out."

It cheered him up to have a good moan, and he was keen to share his good humour with others. He worked with my father at the Gas Producer. One day, a workman cycling past hit a stone and was pitched over the handlebars. As he drew himself to his feet, he was greeted by Harry saying:

"Nah then. That's fower faults. Get up an' try an' go fer a clear round."

It is unlikely that he appreciated this sally, but Harry was pleased with it, for he repeated it for some years thereafter.

Harry suffered from a morbid fear of dogs, and since it was in those days common for dogs to wander about unattended, sometimes in packs, this was no insignificant disability. It was not merely large and aggressive dogs that inspired terror in him. A mere Yorkshire terrier could in his eyes assume Baskervillian qualities not apparent to anyone else. Nor was this fear irrational; in or near Harry's presence, even the mildest, most pampered and most civilized canine was transformed into a slavering maneater. Again and again Harry was jumped upon, harried, bitten and snarled at. His life was one of furtive dog-avoidance.

It was perhaps as well that he was an equable, somewhat fatalistic, man, for there was little enough in his family life to foster a more optimistic outlook or to compensate him for living in a world in which he might at any moment be subjected to sabre-toothed attack. His wife, my Aunt Bessie, was an unprepossessing woman, with a large chin and an unsmiling mien. She spoke little and rarely went out. We were told that she had never learnt to read and write. It may have been that she was somewhat conscious of this. There was always a faint air of dissatisfaction about her, and indeed a profound restlessness. She was, in principle, a working wife, but her employment record was astonishing. She must have had hundreds of jobs, often working in a factory for a day or two at a time before deciding that it did not suit her; whereupon, she moved on. Living with her cannot have been a picnic. They had a child, Maureen, who was several years younger than me and, being female, not of much account so far as I was concerned. She was, however, regarded as more than ordinarily mischievous, being given to such idiosyncratic experiments as drowning tortoises in the lavatory.

Unsurprisingly, then, Harry was one of that great number of working men who spent the greater part of everyday not in his house, but out of doors in his shed. He was especially devoted to his pigeons, whom he cared for with a tenderness that his wife can scarcely have experienced and would certainly not have reciprocated, or even perhaps have greatly welcomed. He would hold them carefully, stroking them lovingly. And, of course, he raced them. Occasionally, I would accompany him to Wolverhampton Low Level Station to watch him and scores of other working men, identically clad in flat caps, mackintoshes and bicycle clips (he cycled everywhere, so slowly that his ability to remain upright struck one as miraculous), loading brown baskets onto trains, so that the birds could be released, in Barmouth it might be, or Rhyl, to fly a hundred miles home. It seemed to me miraculous that they could do this. It still does. It is perhaps even odder that they should choose to return to what was, after all, captivity. Why, I wondered, didn't they simply stay in Barmouth? I have been there several times and, though not entirely free of vulgarities, it is certainly preferable to Wolverhampton. Mostly, though, they returned, and the hours of waiting were anxious indeed. Occasionally, a pigeon would fail to come home, perhaps exhausted, eaten by a cat, or snagged in telegraph wires. These were occasions of some dismay, confirming Harry in his view of life as something rather remote from a bowl of cherries.

My mother's second brother, Harold, also took a sombre, if not apocalyptic, view of life. He was Religious. He did not, of course, go to church, or even chapel, but he took the Watchtower, and was fond of repeating its predictions of doom. We were all condemned, by virtue of irredeemable sin, he would claim, with evident satisfaction, since he was entirely cheerful in face of the coming fires of damnation. Like his brother Harry, he did not allow a profoundly pessimistic view of life to spoil his digestion.

As a young man, he had had a passing resemblance to Ronald Coleman, and had also been, unusually for a Thornsbury, on occasion a snappy dresser. He had been popular, by all accounts, with the girls, and still retained, despite his religiosity, an easy-going charm. He was the gentlest of men and in the end went quite deaf and suffered miserably from a disorder of the middle ear caused by decades of working in a steel-pressing mill. His last years were house-bound and in the end confused. For much of his life, however, he was content to live in the overwhelming presence of his wife, Hazel, to tend his garden, read the "Watchtower" , reflect in amused vein on the prevalence of mortal sin and the approach of doom and draw cartoons which were both skilful and witty.

His religious utterances were not taken seriously by those around him. When his brother Luke died in his early seventies, an event which no one could find it in their hearts wholly to regret, Harold took to musing aloud in the hearse:

"Yo know the dead come back, doe yer?"

33

"Oh bloody 'ell, doe say that! We've only just got rid of 'im."

The hearse was instantly full of happily laughing mourners, to the chagrin of my Aunt Florrie:

"Oh doe laugh! People will see us. It ay right at a funeral."

Harold and his brothers lived a life that was so limited as to be beyond the conception of people living today. None of them ever drove, or used a computer and of the three only Harold ever went abroad, to Austria, towards the end of his life. For Harold at least there were two consolations. The first of these was football. So long as he was able, he took the bus to stand on the terraces at Molyneux, week after week. He was of course convinced that Wolverhampton Wanderers, like all other human institutions, were in a process of inexorable decline, though it was difficult to sustain this view during the fifties, when only Manchester United were serious rivals for the title of best team in England. There was Billy Wright, Bill Slater, Eddy Clamp and the magnificent Ron Flowers, Jimmy Mullen, Norman Deeley and Denis Willshaw; these were the days well before footballers were required to be called Jermaine or Joleon. It was a galaxy, and a team that played a hectic, high-risk brand of football that looks ridiculously naïve in recollection today. It was based on the simple proposition, demonstrated by a boffin called Major Buckley and ruthlessly implemented by the great manager, Stan Cullis, that the quicker you got the ball into the opponents' penalty area, the more you scored. Power and speed were of the essence, with occasional touches of skill from Slater, or the delectable Peter Broadbent, who fulfilled the function, now obsolete, of "schemer". In the end, like many great teams, Wolves failed to adapt in time, and I was there on the day the dinosaurs died, the day they played Harry Nicholson's Spurs. Tottenham Hotspur played the game to a wholly different tempo and melody: a mesmerising one. They frustrated Wolves' cavalry charges by simply denying them possession of the ball, stringing together pass after pass. They won 4-0, to a shocked silence, punctuated by awed applause. Harold was there too. So, he doubtless reflected, he had been right after all.

His other source of contentment was his family. My Auntie Hazel was by far the most beloved of all my relatives. She was a Devonian, who had been diverted to the West Midlands, during the war, though I have never discovered what, if any significant, part she played in Hitler's downfall. My Granddad was the first to see her.

"By, I 'ave seen a big wench," he reported, "by, she is big."

Most people who met Hazel were similarly impressed. Her girth became the stuff of legend. She was very dark and cannot have been more than five feet tall, but she was certainly five feet thick, with immensely fat legs, ending remarkably in suddenly slim ankles. She was coy about her weight: I should guess it varied between 20 and 30 stone, and though she was of a naturally cheerful and optimistic outlook, she could never become reconciled to being fat, or ever find the will to diet.

"I ain't as fat as 'er, am I, me buck," she would whisper, pointing to a lady who would inevitably be by comparison sylph-like. Then, not being given to taking herself too seriously, she would laugh.

I guess she had a natural tendency to put on weight. Her mother was similarly huge, and formidable in other ways: she was a clairvoyant who dominated a household which included both her lover and her discarded husband, taken in when he fell on hard times. Hazel's main problem, however, was not genetic. She simply loved food. Any hour that passed without ingesting food, pre-ferably sweet and creamy, was a desert and a waste. She especially favoured a sort of whipped cream that came out of something like an aerosol; she attributed to this magical weight-reducing pro-perties. She cooked often, and by local standards, well, and she ate a high proportion of what she made, even as she made it. She would maintain that she never picked; the food seeped in through her pores.

Hazel had a fierce temper, as quickly appeased as it was swiftly provoked. Her rages were frequent, but not destructive.

"Yer bloody 'ornet!"

She would yell, as she tripped over the dog, or stamped with bare feet, on one of her son's many toy cars, left on his bedroom floor. To be a dog in Hazel's household was in many ways no great slice of luck. Nothing could persuade her that dogs require regular exercise and a canine diet. They ate what they were given, and lay around, growing fat and smelly, until they were little more than corpulent hearth-rugs. That apart, Hazel, for all her irascibility, was the soul of kindness.

She and Harold – or 'Aral, as she called him – were an oddly assorted couple. She made about five of him: he was small, slight and dapper, she gargantuan; he was quiet, sardonic and humorous, she easily wound up into a storm of temper:

"'E's a bloody daft bugger,"

She would say, after Harold had expounded some detail of eschatology, since for her the end of the world ranked considerably below Sunday lunch in her hierarchy of importance. Yet, they were inseparable. They never, I suppose, had much money. Harold's earnings could not have been large, and Hazel earned only a pittance from a bit of cleaning. The mind boggles at the notion of paying Hazel to clean one's house! She had little time to spare for housework between eating and talking, and in any case found it impossible to bend to anything much below the level of a tabletop. Her house was not therefore in danger of being likened to a new pin. If they were poor, though, their wants were small. They lived in a council house, small, cold and inconvenient, built just after the war. It was enough for them, and they were both by nature disposed to make the best of what they had.

They had also a son, my cousin Roy, born two months after me. Roy, as they say, "took after" his mother, not so much in temperament (though he became more like her in adult life) as in looks. Like her, he was short, dark and rotund. He was also notoriously spoilt. I recall being envious of his cupboards full of toys; it did not occur to me that his possession of them was related to his much greater ability to take care of them. Any toys I had were soon smashed beyond repair. He was also as a small child somewhat liable to acts of unprovoked violence – biting was a favourite mode of attack – that were invariably indulged by his parents, particularly where the victim was me. It was understood that any assault I suffered would have been both provoked and entirely my own fault. There may have been some resentment mixed in that I was the first grandson, and treated with a favour that was not wholly extended to the second. At any rate, I was not often permitted to play with Roy. It was an unwritten rule that, wherever there was an element of competition, he should be permitted to win, and this was not a rule that recommended itself to me. Whenever we did play together, there would be a flare-up. There is photograph in existence of us both armed to the teeth, Roy in his Mounties uniform, me with bow and arrow, and the sword from which I was never willingly parted. It is a fair bet that we would have inflicted injury on each other within minutes of the photo's being taken.

As Roy grew beyond his earliest childhood, though still indulged, he became more relaxed and amenable. This may have been partly due to the absence of any pressure of expectations upon him. His appearances at primary school, despite the fact that it was two hundred yards from his front gate, were sporadic and uninvolved. His mother was not an early riser, and it was not to be expected that he would leave the house of his own volition, or without breakfast. He therefore suffered from the eccentric insistence of the Education Committee that the school day began at 9 AM, a time which rarely found him or his mother conscious. It was therefore no surprise that he effortlessly failed the 11-plus and attended – occasionally – the local secondary modern school. It was a further deterrent to him that the school was improbably distant from home – at least half a mile, and up quite a steep hill. His lack of academic distinction therefore persisted, and he sank at once into the bottom set, where he happily remained, learning little beyond the basics, and spent a good deal of time assisting in the cultivation of the school gardens. The school took the enlightened view that if children were ineducable, they might as well learn nothing in the open air. Nowadays, such a record of non-education would be impossible. Then, it hardly mattered. If you did not go to the grammar school, you were still certain of employment, usually in the West Midlands skilled employment.

Roy was not of course ineducable; it was merely that the school and the school curriculum were not to his taste. This was, I think, true of many of us. The commonest comment on school reports was, inevitably. "he shows no interest," ignoring any onus there might have been on the teacher to elicit interest. Roy educated himself, with the help of his dad, in the things in which he was interested. The first of these was aeroplanes: he had a collection of hundreds of model planes, assembled from intricate and, to me, perfectly intractable kits, with loving care and some skill. He could identify any plane that had ever flown, and had an encyclopaedic command of their detailed specifications; he would regale me with this information at the least provocation, or none, having, ironically given his distaste for school, a strongly didactic bent. Like, presumably, his unavailing teachers, he was convinced of your duty to absorb whatever information he happened to be interested in imparting. Later, he transferred this intense and in its way scholarly focus to the study of the internal combustion engine, whereupon he would tell you all you had never felt the need to know about cars. He also became an expert photographer, with a well-equipped darkroom. He was a natural enthusiast, collector and student; but there was no place for him in school as it was then organized.

The three of them, Harold, Roy and Hazel, formed a perfectly contented and self-sufficient family unit. None of them went out in the evenings much; they preferred home, each other's company, the television and the fireside. Later, when Roy learned to drive, they would take little trips together, or visit Hazel's place of origin in the West Country. Roy was, I suspect, so secure in the love of his parents that it simply never occurred to him that his failure at school should be experienced by him as something humiliating or demeaning. He really did not care.

Hazel and my eldest Aunt, Florrie, did not get on. Indeed, they rarely met, though Hazel and Harold had lived for some time with Florrie in the early part of their marriage. How they managed this I cannot imagine. I recall Harold when on nightshift coming to sleep during the day at our house, as an alternative to Florrie's, on the premise that we the children would be out and the house quiet. Florrie's house was somewhat superior to those in which the rest of us lived, in that it was semi-detached, and had a drive, rather than an entry. We understood in some indefinable way that these attributes made her residence a cut above. However, the house was tiny: it had a reasonable number of rooms, but each of them individually was both very small and inconceivably crammed: with photographs, reproductions of bad paintings, mirrors, bric a brac and souvenirs of their own and other people's holidays. A plaster ring bore the improbable legend "Ad Assisi Andai"; a model of Blackpool tower was witness to a more credible visit; postcards recalled golden days at Rhyl or Prestatyn; wild ducks flew in ascending and descending formation over the heads of ceramic spaniels and cats made of plaster-of-paris. A three-piece suite grouped around a fireplace occupied a kind of clearing in this forest of eccentricity, and there my Aunt Florrie would sit, knitting as she chatted.

Knitting was the revenge the women of that generation took on the rest of the world for the misfortune of being born female in a man's world. We all wore knitted socks, cardigans and pullovers, often in patterns chosen for their very bizarreness, so as to display the skill of the knitter. One might therefore be required to present oneself to the world in a green pullover emblazoned with a purple toad or an octopus, or dolphin, or in a cardigan in that especially excruciating assault on the senses known as "Fairisle." The shape of these garments rarely survived their first wash. Generally, they rode up at the back, and sagged at the front, so that it was possible to be exposed at the rear for nine to ten inches above the waist, but at the front to have wool extending downwards almost to the knees. One felt an idiot. How I longed for machine-made woollens, or for summer, when the command "put yer pullover on," might not be the hateful accompaniment of one's invariably late preparations for school. Both my mother and Hazel continued knitting as old ladies, at which point they were adding to the already considerable woes of Rumanian orphans by inflicting on them a humiliation of which even the wicked Ceausescu was not guilty.

My Aunt Florrie was a wholly benign being. She presided over her packed living room like a round and smiling Buddha; she was perhaps a little too ready to dispense advice, but the more obvious reason for her lack of affinity with Hazel was to be found in her husband:

"Bill!"

Hazel would exclaim, with magnificent contempt and in the absolute certainty that nothing else whatever need be said. The single syllable was in itself enough. It was less a name for her than an oath. She would never have uttered the monosyllable, "shit!" Had she done so, it would have contained no more distaste than that with which she invested the apparently more innocent "Bill!" "Bill!" No more need be said; the syllable itself was enough, in Hazel's view, to explain the animosity that lay behind it. "Bill!" my mother would reply, and that was enough to establish an understanding.

I did not know what lay behind this hostility, which was never explained. I did not, and do not, believe the story about him cutting off his trigger finger to avoid conscription. That would be an act of such cold-blooded courage that I think most men would be incapable of it. The only concrete accusation that I can remember being made about Bill was that he was somewhat uxorious. He worked, as a bread-deliveryman, but nevertheless went shopping, apparently willingly, with his wife, and, worse still, helped with the household chores. It was certainly true that the three of them, Florrie, Bill and their daughter Rosemary, were an unusually close and loving trio. But Bill's faults as a loving husband and a doting father, were surely evidence of eccentricity, not depravity. I had no more objection to him than that consisting in the mere fact of his being an adult and therefore ex officio part of the opposition. He was fond of bad jokes, but he always smelled pleasantly of new-baked bread. It was sometimes said, sternly, that he was fond of women, and this again marked him out as somewhat unusual among the men of Wednesfield. It was only many years after his death that I learned from my sister that he was actually a sexual pest: not virile enough to be a predator, but persistent enough to be a distasteful nuisance. My mother also noted, with scepticism, the improbable regularity with which he claimed to have "won" the Christmas turkey. Florrie, it is safe to say, would have been deeply humiliated had she guessed any of this. She was the closest we came to being "religious". She attended the Wesleyan Chapel in the Village assiduously, and made cushions for it, to ease the suffering of pious bums. If she had known what Bill was up to on his bread round, her world would have fallen apart. She was fortunately entirely unaware of any of her husband's faults, real or reported.

These then were the Gods of my childhood, the people among whom I lived for the first decade and a half of my life. We almost never came together as a family, except at funerals. The only family "do" I remember was Rosemary's twenty-first birthday party, an occasion my mother took as evidence of Florrie's distressing tendency to entertain "big ideas." If we did not assemble formally, however, there can have been few weeks in which, especially while my grandparents were still alive, we did not see one or more of my aunts and uncles. I doubt if it ever occurred to them to wonder whether they much liked each other. Like the rest of life, family was something you got on with as best you could.

Not all of my family lived locally. My paternal grandmother was alive until I was 18. She lived in a village called Blennerhasset, a few miles to the North of Bassenthwaite Lake in Cumbria, in a terraced cottage which is now called "Four Winds." It had no name then, and no need of any. It was Jinnie's House; everyone knew that. There were green studs on the oak door, which is still there, though the house itself looks alarmingly gentrified. There was a strip of cobbles outside, and growing through it a large oak tree, in which woodpigeons perched, making what seemed to me an extraterrestrial noise early on summer mornings: soft, but insistent, and impossible for a town boy to sleep through. The cottage was made of stone, with implausibly thick walls, as it seemed to me then, used as I was to city brick. There were two rooms downstairs, with a large pantry, and two up, though a third bed could be put in an alcove, divided off by a curtain. I lay there, more contentedly than anywhere else in my life, and still recall it as a place of lost content. It was not advisable to drink too much late at night. The lavatory was some distance away, beyond a large chicken-pen. The cottage was austere, but clean, airy, with a safe feeling about it from a sense it had of having been securely lived in for several centuries.

We did not visit my granny till I was 11. I do not know precisely why, but I suspect that when they first met, she and my mother were mutually unimpressed with each other. I think, too, that there may have been some jealousy that, on being demobbed, my father chose to go to his fiancé rather than head North to his mother. Granny Singleton was slender and somewhat refined, and spoke in the quiet, often humorous, lilt of the Borders. She had lived on a farm for much of her life, and had the farmer's wife's skill of making something delicious out of any scrap of food. Her pastry was delectable, her home-made Cumberland sausage defied belief. Her manner was gentle, but she had had the steel to leave her husband, taking her two young sons, and walk twenty miles to her brother's house to announce that she had come to live. My grandfather had been – may still have been – a farmworker, who apparently specialized in advising on irrigation, not usually a pressing need in Westmoreland, over in the coastal stretch of Cumbria beyond Pillar, where Seascale now is. I do not know the reason for the break, but I suspect that it had something to do with drink, as most things did in my family. He was, I have since learnt, an alcoholic, though a very intelligent man.

Granny Singleton, then, lived with her brother, my uncle (in fact, great uncle) Bob, whose surname, peculiarly, was Dusnap, which I have not otherwise encountered. He was when I met him already in his early 70's, rosy-cheeked, slow-moving and genial. He was hunched of the back and partly paralyzed down his right side, as a result of having hit a concealed tree-stump while out ploughing. At the time of his accident, he had been a young man, engaged to be married, but had insisted on breaking off the engagement on realizing that he would be permanently disabled. By repute, the young woman was still eager to marry, but he felt it would be wrong in principle to begin married life as a burden. He showed no signs of unhappiness or resentment at the hand life had dealt him. He viewed the world with tolerant amusement, and moved at his own pace:

"God made time, and he made plenty of it."

This was a standard Cumbrian response to any suggestion of hurry, and it was Uncle Bob's guiding principle. He had built up a small newspaper business, though he had, of course, no shop. His papers would arrive by van from Carlisle station at 4 AM, and he would sort them into the order of his stately progress around the local towns, villages and hamlets, and off he would drive.

It was my great delight, with my sister Pauline, to accompany Uncle Bob on his paper round. He had never taken a driving test, nor is it conceivable that he could ever have passed one, since he had only one hand, the left, with which to drive, the right being virtually useless. On a fine day, he would hang his limp right hand out of the driver's side window, as though signalling – a thing which he never did. He considered it unnecessary, since he always travelled by the same route, at the same speed (a little faster than walking pace); we rarely encountered other vehicles. When we did so, they were usually tractors, proceeding with the same absence of unseemly haste. Stops were frequent, often entailing leaving the car parked, window still open, in the middle of a narrow lane or, on occasions, at a road junction. The delivery of each newspaper was a small social occasion.

"wi' it renn, today, then, Bob?"

A minute of meditative silence would ensue:

"I dinna think," he would at last reply.

"This is our Alan's wee lass and bairn," he would add.

"Oh aye, fine big chil'en," would be the reply, and then a sweet, pastry or piece of sponge would be offered, and eagerly accepted, thereby ensuring that we became even bigger, if not finer. After about four hours of this we were ready for our lunch, taken in a pub on the outskirts of Wigton. We made, I have subsequently discovered, a somewhat mixed impression locally. My sister and I were perceived, not unnaturally, to be so solemn and withdrawn that people worried about us.

Both my grandmother and my Uncle Bob have now been dead for over 40 years, and I do not know which, if any, of my relatives survive in what was Westmoreland. My father's younger brother, Thomas, lived in Aspatria, and would be over 80 by now. I went back to Blennerhasset some seven or eight years ago, and it seemed somehow ordinary. My grandmother's cottage was still there; so were the shop, and the bridge over the Beck, that has been known to flood. It was no longer the paradise I thought it when I was 11, when it was my first experience of being in the real countryside, as opposed to the reclaimed waste-heaps on which I played. I have never forgotten my first enchanted sight of Blennerhasset, or the journey to it. Probably, everyone recalls the moment they first looked down on Windermere. Starved as I was, though unaware of it, of beauty, that first view awoke in me a new sense of the intensity of emotion the natural world was capable of evoking. From then on, I was a Black Country lad, but an exile in the place of my birth and upbringing.

Dads and Uncles

Men were different in 1953: apart,
Somehow. They lived, not in houses,
But in factories and streets, and clubs,
And smelled of tar, the smoke of fags
And sweat, wearing large deflated overalls,
Bulky as leather balls empty of air:
Dads and uncles, occasional bulky
Presences that filled the house
And occupied the warm spot
By the fire, but not for long, never
For long. They gave their rulings,
Administered their punishments,
Allocated their resources, went away
Into the serious adult world that waited,
Expectant as a hungry cat, ill defined
As fog; these were men that fought,
Had seen service in legendary lands,
Against the unimaginable,
And had not died. Having nothing else
To do, they had now come back,
To labour in the factory down the road,
And father children they would rarely see
By women with whom they felt no ease.

Crimes and punishments

The Regal Cinema

Quite early in my childhood, I began to acquire from the local library the "Just William" books of Richmal Crompton. I did not so much enjoy them, as regard them as a model of boyhood. William Brown, with his "Outlaws" and his dog, Jumble, seemed to me to lead precisely the kind of childhood I would have liked to be having: adventurous, lawless, and fundamentally safe. Whatever misdemeanours William commits incurred no serious risk, such is the all-enveloping security of his prosperous bourgeois home, with his frequently disapproving, but always loving and supremely competent mother. She was, of course – and this was a vital point of difference – very definitely "mother" and not "Mum", and the extra syllable conveyed a whole world of expectation of feminine behaviour. William's mother did not aim blows at his head, chase him with a poker, or utter the dreaded

words, "Yerdad'll give yo a good 'idin' when 'e cums whum."
When apprehended in crime, William was sent to bed, or had
pocket money withdrawn. Without realizing it, I deeply envied his
world of affluent emotional security. I was as lawless as William,
but the consequences of being caught could be, and often were,
more direct and more painful.

I was not part of any such settled group as "The Outlaws." I had
no dog like Jumble, and it is inconceivable that I would have had
friends with such distinctively middle-class names as Douglas
or Henry. Such a creature as Violet Elizabeth Bott has, to this
day, not been seen in Wednesfield. My friends sported names
like Michael, Ian, Gerald and Royston. We ranged far and wide
around Wednesfield, but the centre of our activities was usually
"The Park". This was King George's Park and Playing Fields:
neither particularly large nor especially exotic, but to us as foreign
and as pregnant with adventure as any terrain travelled by Alan
Quartermain or Professor Challenger. This was our Lost World,
our undiscovered Africa, conveniently close and, in summer, often
with an ice-cream van to be found outside the gates. Here were
savannahs, jungles, impenetrable swamps, trackless deserts and
staunchly defended oases.

In sober fact, the park was – and it is not the first country in
history of which this is true – divided into three parts. Furthest in
distance from my home was "the field" – a relatively large and
monotonous stretch of grass marked out into some half a dozen
football fields. Two of these were, on one memorable and somewhat lunatic occasion merged to provide a venue for a game of
what we were told was "Shinty". This appeared to be a hybrid of
lacrosse and Australian rules football, played by psychopaths,
without benefit of the Geneva Convention or Queensbury Rules.
We wondered at it, but were told that the players were Irish, as
though that were in itself sufficient explanation. We had not realized the Irish were locally so numerous, for the field appeared
crammed with a stick-wielding mob. Usually, the activity was
more sedate. The best, i.e. least sloping and most pebble-free,

pitch was reserved for Wednesfield Football Club. This was a body of men with significant local prestige, not that that was always a good thing, since to have prestige is often to attract challenge. In our teens we all knew a boy called Stephen who played for their junior side. It became a point of honour with us to challenge him to a fight, a challenge rendered all the more attractive by his being, albeit nippy and skilful, small and unaggressive. His life must have been a misery.

The field received no attention from any groundsmen, other than the marking of the pitches on matchdays. The surface would not have satisfied the more delicately skilful sort of footballer. Fortunately, such people barely existed in those days. The football was, in those stern times, a large lump of leather inflated to the hardness of concrete. The surface absorbed water, gaining exponentially in weight during a game on a wet Saturday or Sunday. The main requisite of any player was the improbable mass of muscle required to propel this object more than, say, thirty yards. Our hero was a footballer, famous in his day, called Ron Flowers. Ron was blonde, six feet tall, and built like a trainee gorilla. He was a great player for Wolves and England, but his party-piece was to stride through what is now called the "midfield" and propel the ball high over the goal to rebound from the roof of the stand and disappear entirely out of the stadium and into the grounds of the Molyneux hotel. This was by no means an attempt to score; it was simply a demonstration, eagerly awaited, of immense physical prowess. No one else in England could do this. Certainly, no one who appeared on "The Field" came close to doing it. Our own puny games rarely moved much beyond the centre circle, as our feeble hacks moved the ball hardly more than a car's length. The grown-up matches were less static. What seemed to us remarkable was how much time the ball spent in the air, travelling vast distances, to be met by heads risking instant concussion. Anyone who has not headed a 1950's "caseball" extracted from the mud has not known the true douceur de la vie. When journalists wrote, "Lofthouse scored with a stunning header," they were guilty of no hyperbole.

Like much else in those happy days, sports journalism had a pre-
dictability we found reassuring. Headers could be relied upon to
be "stunning," literally, as well as metaphorically, just as anyone
who could kick straight with the wrong foot could rely upon
being described as having an "educated left foot." Educated right
feet did not exist. Full-backs were conventionally "barrel-chested"
and wingers "tricky," or "elusive," or both. Defences were either
"rock-like," or leaked "like a sieve," the improbable transition
from one state to another, often within the same game, usually
remaining unexplained. Defenders who could not tackle were
invariably "cultured." Injured players were "courageous," as
indeed they had to be, since there were no substitutes, and to play
with ten men was to invite "gallant" defeat, following "stubborn"
resistance. Ineptitude on the part of the goalkeeper was described
as "a despairing dive," and penalties were conventionally "hotly
disputed." Accurate passes were "measured with a slide-rule,"
oblivious of the fact that the slide rule is an instrument not of
measurement, but of computation. This stock of cliché lodged in
our minds and, without our realizing it, instilled in us something
approaching an ethic.

The Field contained nothing other than football pitches, apart
from a single, rather narrow, strip of concrete, presumably 22
yards long, which was meant to be, I think, a cricket pitch. We
rarely played on it, since to do so was even more hazardous than
playing on the hard-packed soil of the football pitches, all of
which were worn to the consistency of beaten clay long before the
start of summer. A ball accurately pitched on the concrete would
gather pace and beat any conceivable stroke we might make; if
slightly short of a length it would threaten the knuckles or even
the teeth. It should be pointed out that we played with cricket-
balls of compounded cork, and with neither pads nor batting
gloves. Only a fool would ever play forward: we remained
discretely on the back foot and flailed cross-batted. Any ball
which failed to pitch on the concrete, as the majority did, simply
lodged in the long grass, usually failing to reach the batsman at
all. The Field was almost entirely the preserve of boys. Girls did

not, in those far-off days, play football, and I do not recall them
gathering for impromptu games of rounders, as we did for
football. The minimum number for a game was four: two sides of
two, with jackets for goals and no touchlines. Lacking precise
delineation, our pitches were fertile ground for dispute: over, for
example, whether a ball had gone out for a "corner", or whether a
shot had or had not gone over the imaginary bar. Much time
would be spent picking sides. Being large, I often got to pick. This
was helpful insurance against the dire humiliation of being the last
man selected; worst of all was when the two sides were uneven.
Occasionally, the selector would come to the last man, often an
unfortunate called, ludicrously, Jonathan, eye him contemptuously
and say,

"You can have him. We'll have kick-off."

Next to The Field was "The Lane", where many of us had our
initiation into the forbidden pleasures of tobacco and Bulmer's
cider. This was a narrow pathway that led from the car-park of a
public house behind the gardens of a street of houses and finally
wound its way between two iron fences that divided "The Field,"
from the playing field, which was the core of "The Park." This
had the usual collection of amusements from which the fertile
imagination could conjure improbable dangers: swings, climbing
frames, slides, see-saws a sand-pit, a roundabout and a weird
construction we called "The Witch's Hat," which was a sort of
drunkenly lurching roundabout.

It was not the habit of parents in the nineteen-fifties to supervise
children – above the age of about five – at play. Few, however,
could have been under any illusion as to the forms which our play
was likely to take. The Park was the venue for stunts of appalling
danger, as it now seems to me. For example, the correct technique
on the swings was to fly upwards as high as possible, then to leap
from the seat just as it reached its apogee. With the roundabout,
the custom was to hang on to the handles, spin the roundabout as
fast as possible, then allow the centrifugal force to carry one's

body parallel to the ground. This worked better when smaller children or girls were imprisoned on the seats, so that the rapid motion of the roundabout was accompanied by helpless screaming. The see-saw was a kind of duel: the objective was suddenly to leap from the seat, so that your partner was left to crash unexpectedly to the ground, producing a satisfying concussion in a delicate area. The sand pit was a venue for long-jumping competitions, rendered more interesting by its three foot depth and the excellent chance of rendering oneself or others unconscious on landing. In a sense most dangerous of all was the paddling pool: a dire stretch of unspeakably filthy water, patrolled by hairy water-boatmen of spectacular size. In summer, we attempted to swim in its eighteen inches of stagnant filth.

"The Lane" was the venue for different sorts of misdemeanour. For half of its length, it offered concealment, and was therefore where many of us had out first fag or, in the case of the lucky few, our first sweaty and malodorous sexual experience. It was not, though, a thoroughfare to be approached without some trepidation and some attempt at reconnaissance. The chances of suddenly encountering the Beeson gang or the Laker gang were quite high, and escape in a confined space would be impossible. A beating would then follow, usually accompanied by some form of humiliation, redoubled if one were soft enough to cry.

The third part of "The Park" consisted of tennis courts and bowling greens, surrounded by ornamental gardens. The courts were for adults, though we occasionally, and briefly, ventured on to them through a gap in the wire fence. This was an act of defiance, rather than a serious effort at occupation, since we were invariably chased away by a zealous groundsman:

"Geroff. Yer buggers,"

He would cry, and we would flee, sometimes pausing to hurl a stone or two. The greens were immaculately kept, but the ornamental gardens were, as I now suspect, unconvincing: there were wide lawns, surrounded by privet hedges and flowering borders, yellow with marigolds in spring. We viewed the lawns with some cupidity, since they offered a far more inviting surface for cricket than either The Field or the concrete pitch. No game, however, lasted more than twenty minutes: we would see the park-keeper's hat bobbing over the hedge, and it would be time to escape. Getting caught by the parkies was not a fate to be endured. It would lead, following a cuff round the head, to something official, such as being hauled to one's front door and being handed over for later punishment.

Predictably, this danger added the spice of adventure to our days in the Park. It now seems to me that there was a sort of Geneva Convention informally in existence between the two warring factions, ourselves and the parkies. They seldom, so far as I am aware, simply reported on you; they had actually physically to apprehend you, and their sphere of authority did not extend beyond the perimeter of the park. Once you were through the gate, it was understood that you were away and free. The object of much of our activity was therefore to provoke pursuit, but to evade arrest. One favourite trick was to run across the lawns and dive headfirst onto the top of the surrounding hedge. The springy privet would enable you to somersault spectacularly onto the soft flowerbed below, sometimes leaving behind an area of devastated vegetation. Invariably, this provoked the rage of the parkies, who were of course restricted to more formal means of egress. They would pursue hotly. Sometimes, two at a time, they would seek to block escape routes. This almost never worked. We knew every hole in every hedge, every gap in every fence.

One Easter, I remember, Mickey and I spent weeks building a treehouse, bit by bit, in a section of the park that was adjacent to some wasteland, beside the canal. There, there were a couple of concrete air-raid shelters left over from the war; no one had bothered to remove them, or to seal them up, and they made excellent hiding-places. From there, we could slip through the fence into the park and, in emergency, as quickly out. I think we must have done rather more damage than usual, because this was the only occasion on which I recall our being "reported." The Parkies had broken the terms of our unwritten convention so far as to inform the police of our activities and, worse, our names. The subsequent arrival of a uniformed constable at our front door was not the happiest occasion I remember, but it was preferable to the subsequent encounter with my father, who smacked away contentedly.

It must not be thought that the whole of my youth was dedicated to lawlessness. My external adventures were essentially interruptions to a settled habit of bookishness, and my preferred occupation was to curl up in a chair with a book, and a quarter of boiled sweets ready to hand. There were always books in the house: not that we owned very many, but my father read avidly and was a weekly visitor to the library. He read a great deal of rubbish: mainly westerns, but also some rather better comic literature: P.G.Wodehouse was a great favourite, as was Damon Runyan, and he would often read aloud passages that struck him especially; Hemingway and Somerset Maugham were also acceptable, and Raymond Chandler was particularly admired. I read, I think, all of these and more from an early age. I think it is true to say that I cannot remember a time when I could not read. Certainly, I recollect being taught the alphabet at school, but with a certain mystification: why did I need to sit in a large and draughty room, with what seemed like hundreds of other children, smelling of cooling toast, in order to be taught things I already knew?

The opening of the Wednesfield branch library was a great event. It is tucked in, opposite St. Thomas' church, beside the canal bridge. Conveniently, it has flower-beds below the bridge; often, these provided a soft landing, as we leapt from the bridge in order to circumvent the queues that formed at opening time on Saturday morning. Children now would scarcely believe that we queued, and attempted to jump the queue, in order to get the best books before they were taken. On the day of the grand opening, we were taken from school, lining up neatly outside the library, to be issued

with four brown dockets: two for fiction and two for non-fiction. I
remember a vague disappointment that when I got to the shelves
there was little left: certainly no William, or Famous Five, or Billy
Bunter. I cannot quite remember what I got, but I think it was
either then or soon after that I borrowed a children's version of
the Morte d'Arthur. I read it avidly, just as I did the improving
literature I was given for Christmas and at birthdays: Lamb's
"Tales from Shakespeare," or the Arabian Nights in a carefully
expurgated version. I read all the usual children's classics,
including those, like "Wuthering Heights," or "Uncle Tom's
Cabin," that were certainly not directed primarily at the very
young. I devoured "Treasure Island," "Lorna Doone," "The
Coral Island," and many of the girls' classics as well. I was
especially impressed by "The Children of the New Forest," which
I read as a kind of sylvan, parent-free idyll. The terrors and
dangers of that perilous century struck me not at all. I largely
enjoyed "The Three Musketeers," too, though in the end I felt it
had a ruthlessness that made it definitely unBritish; the execution
of Milady in particular struck me as not the sort of expedient
Peter May would have stooped to.

From the age of about ten, Mickey and I were regular weekly
visitors to the library. He borrowed as many books as I did (two
fiction and two non fiction a week) but his penchant was for
action, rather than reflection. Thus he never left the library
without having first let down the tires on the librarian's bicycle.

I had two favourite non-fiction books. One was a set of quiz
questions and answers, which was so magnificently dogmatic that
it represented a standard of certainty that ever since I have longed
to recapture. "What is the Greatest Painting in the World?"
Answer: "The Last Supper," by Leonardo da Vinci, in Santa Maria
Delle Grazie in Milan. There followed a description of the
disintegration of the painting, due to Leonardo's ill-conceived
experiments with fresco technique, that left me wondering what
was so great about it if it couldn't even contrive to stay on the
wall. The answer to: "Who was the world's greatest magician?"

– Harry Houdini – was perhaps less debatable, but there too the account of his unfortunate demise seemed to me to remove the gloss from what might otherwise have been impeccable performance. I reflected, too, that Captain Webb might have been better advised to stick to Channel-swimming, given his misfortune in the Hellespont. These troubling assertions apart, I gleaned a great many facts which throughout my life have stood me in good stead, enabling me to appear far more erudite on a great range of subjects than I actually am on any. I know, for example, that all English thoroughbreds are descended from the Darley Arabian, the Byerley Turk and the Godolphin, I know that the Stradivari, the Guarneri and the Amati were a dab hand at fiddles and lived in Cremona, and I know that Rutherford split the atom. I know thousands of things; more importantly, I was early on inducted into the view that it is fun to know things.

My other favourite non-fiction book similarly combined hard fact, or what appeared to be hard fact, with trenchant opinion. This was Arthur Mee's "Kings and Queen of England." Arthur Mee left the reader in little doubt that the history of England was, unequivocally, a Good Thing: something to be admired and applauded, rather than analysed. The title of his book: "London: Heart of Empire and Wonder of the World" gives something of a clue to his characteristic tone. He was, I think, an autodidact, and he wrote for others of that kind. For him, history was a branch of literature, rather than a social science, and there is no hint of any ambition to transmit "skills," whether deliberately or inadvertently. There are characters, and there are stories, and the stories have a moral. Elizabeth's speech at Tilbury is a predictable highlight: the plucky Queen standing up to the Spanish bully and triumphing through virtue and the support of the ordinary people. The daughter of Henry VIII might perhaps have been slightly surprised to find herself held up for admiration as a kind of proto-democrat, but no matter. The point was that the story of England was one of progress and the gradual revelation, unsurprising to some, that though England might lose its way for a time – the regrettable business over General Gordon was a case in point

– she would always triumph in the end, because God was on her side. To ensure that the moral of the narrative was not lost, Arthur Mee ended the narrative of each reign with explicit moralizing. Stephen was "A brave warrior, but a bad king," John was simply bad and it served him right that he died of a surfeit of lampreys, Coeur de Lion and Henry V were great men and great heroes, with the minor blemish that they both spent hardly any time in England; George iii was not a good king; after all, he spoke to trees and lost America, with the assistance of Lord North. I loved this, and it has been a disappointment of maturity to realise that moralizing about the past is one of the most pointless of activities.

I lived much of my childhood, therefore, in a twilight world which was half-fiction and half highly romanticized fact. I had, and have never had, any hobbies other than reading. I was occasionally persuaded by friends to go fishing, but found it consisted of long periods of tedium, punctuated by episodes of squalid and revolting cruelty. I hated it, as I have always hated any form of cruelty to animals. Much of my imaginary life was focused, then as now, on sport. I was given, at the age of about eight, an "Encyclopaedia of Sport." It was a Christmas Present, the first I opened that year. I was so immediately engrossed by it that it was not until afternoon that I opened any other, apart from the obligatory Fry's selection box. It contained a brief history of each sport, lists of significant achievements, such as Wimbledon and Football League championships, important statistics and potted biographies of great sportsman. I was immediately taken by the lives of the great cricketers. The Honourable F.S. Jackson (Harrow, Cambridge University, Yorkshire and England), I saw, had died on the day that I was born. Surely that established a link between us, suggesting that I was his successor, rather as one Dalai Lama succeeded another. In 1905, he had captained England against Australia, headed the batting and bowling averages and won the toss five times. That was a level of achievement for which I was prepared, in my youthful modesty, to settle. I noted with disapproval that Jackson virtually never played subsequently, being occupied with frivolities, such as being a Conservative MP and governing Bengal.

I learned that Hobbs (J.B.) – the positioning of the initials is crucial – had scored 61,237 runs in first-class cricket, more than anyone else, though Woolley (F.E) had scored almost as many and taken over 2000 wickets. Hobbs, by comparison, was a slacker. I ranged over every sport: from Joe Payne to Lester Piggott and from Ronald Poulton-Palmer to Mlle Suzanne Lenglen, though the Mlle was a bit of a puzzle, since it appeared to be un-pronounceable.

Greater by far than any of these historical sportsman, however, even greater than the nonpareil C.B.Fry himself (this was long before the discovery that Fry had posed naked as a young man for gay pornography) was the Great Wilson (not to be confused with Harold). Wilson would have thought little of Fry's feat of nipping out of a test match to break the world long jump record, before going on to play in the Cup Final. Apart from the regrettable solecism of having been born in Yorkshire, Wilson had all the characteristics of the ideal British hero; he was of a type with T.E.Lawrence or John Hanning Speke. He was, firstly, completely sexless, though naturally devastatingly attractive to women; he was supremely competent at everything he did; and he was wildly eccentric. He dressed in a black singlet and shorts, lived in a cave and ate only berries and nuts. This diet, and a life of spectacular austerity (he was like one of those characters in the Mahabharata who occasionally pop off for thirteen years or so to practise "extreme austerities" in a forest) preserved his physical fitness and gave him apparently eternal youth. He claimed to have been born in a cave in 1795, which would have made him, at the zenith of his fame, comfortably older than Stanley Matthews. I cannot now remember what comic he appeared in – it may have been the Wizard or the Hotspur. An attempt to google him secured only an entry for the writer A.N.Wilson, who I fear is conspicuously not the right man.

Much of my life, then, was lived in the imagination. When I played cricket, I did so, not as myself, but first as Denis Compton and, later, as Garfield Sobers. I even tried to imitate Sobers' characteristic prowl to the wicket, succeeding only in impersonating a drunk with rickets. When I played football, I was Dixie Dean and Ron Flowers; when I ran, I was the Great Wilson. When we fought imaginary battles, I was Richard the Lionheart or Charlie Upham VC and Bar; when we organized scouting parties to spy on the local factories, I was Biggles or Bulldog Drummond, oblivious of the singularly nasty characteristics these preux chevaliers displayed. I recall especially a tale in which Biggles, heavily disguised, is making his way through an Alpine village in Germany. The description, though rudimentary, is idyllic. The neat chalets are hung with brightly coloured baskets, the snow-capped mountains gleaming in the sunshine behind them in the distance. Biggles reflects sourly on the inhabitants:

"God," he sagely opines, "What complete swine they must all be."

I was of course, just as sublimely oblivious of the homoerotic implications of so much of this literature, even of Raffles and his young pal, Bunny. All were brave, manly and honourably dedicated to the extirpation of foreigners.

My friends were, I think, mostly rather less bookish than I was, though we all read and exchanged the same comics. It is one of my regrets that, having moved away from the Black Country as soon as practical, I had no idea what eventually became of my earliest friends until recent months, when I have met Mickey a few times to tour the scenes of our youthful triumphs. I heard from my mother years ago that a friend, Foxy, from grammar school, had died young, killed in a traffic accident. That apart, I know nothing of most of them, even whether they are still alive. It is one of the peculiarities of my life that each phase, once ended, has been completely closed. Looking back, it feels like a succession of existences, rather than one coherent life.

My collection of friends (one could not call them a "circle")would now have been more remarkable for what they were not than what they were. My friends included, of course, no girls. It was unthinkable for any boy over the age of about four to play with the girls and in school the girls sat on one side of the room, the boys on the other. The mutual contempt felt for each other by the sexes was deep and all-encompassing. I had no black friends; no one did. We occasionally saw black, though not Asian, people, but we did not know where they lived, or where they went to school. We called them "chockies," and felt no hostility towards them, and not much curiosity. They were not part of our world. They were rumoured to eat catfood, which we regarded as eccentric, but not culpable. My mother and Aunt Hazel once or twice muttered that "they were not as clean as we are," but we took little note of that. Given the attitude of both of them towards housework, it seemed improbable, and not very important, that there were deeper levels of untidiness and general dirt that could exist. None of my friends' parents owned a house or, until very late in the fifties, a car, and we were the first family in our street to own a television. We got it, as many people did, for the Coronation. The neighbours came in, and expressed delight that the youthful Queen could be dimly discerned through a grey and flickering mist. I vaguely remember thinking that the voices that emerged from the box were strange. No one in Wednesfield spoke like Richard Dimbleby. I put this down to the distorting effects of transmission over a long distance and supposed that if I, too, spoke over the telly, I would sound like Richard Dimbleby. None of my friends' fathers was unemployed; no one had been in prison; no one took, or had heard of, drugs. The world we lived in then was far more homogeneous than any that exists now, and if there was an underclass, we never heard of it, or saw it.

My best friend was Micky, and from the age of 5 to about 14 we were more or less inseparable, even after the eleven-plus took us in different directions. Micky was big and blonde , handsome, and too lazy to be more than average in most things: at school, at football and cricket and in his approach to life, which was easy-going. He was remarkable mainly for his voice, which was especially loud and booming. It was, my mother said, a "foghorn," oddly since I do not imagine she had ever heard a real foghorn in her life spent as far away from the sea as in England it is possible to be. Mickey patrolled the streets and canals of Wednesfield with me, roamed the slagheaps of Bacca's end, went to Wolves' matches when we could afford it. He was, I suspect, slightly more provident than I, or perhaps had more pocket-money. Later on, we both did paper-rounds, in my case not for long. He always had, as I did not, funds with which in the autumn to purchase ample supplies of penny bangers which we lit before posting them through letter-boxes. We both collected, he more assiduously than I, cigarette-cards of famous footballers, and he could quote the career statistics of such obscure players as Len Duquemin or Johnny Atyeo, whose names I could barely pronounce. In his own football, Mickey was not endowed with great skill or speed, but he made himself a respected opponent, because he operated on the principle that if you saw anything moving you should kick it, in case it might be the ball. He possessed a powerful right foot, contact with which was far better avoided. He tended therefore to be picked, in our impromptu games, about as quickly as I was. I was a bit quicker and slightly more skilled, but had less appetite for physical contact. Once – only once – we played in a proper game on a marked out pitch, with goalposts and nets. I cannot remember the occasion; we must have been trialling for a club side. Nothing came of it. I did little, as did Mickey, except that he received the ball on the edge of our opponents' penalty area and let fly with a powerful right-foot shot. It thundered from the cross-bar, to my immense relief. It would have been insufferable had he scored. "Oh bad luck," I shouted, with an odious pretence of sympathy. To my astonishment, he was elated.

"I've done it," he cried, "I've achieved my life ambition. I've 'it the bar!"

Fortunate being, to have so modest an aspiration, so soon achieved.

Mickey's dad was a slightly abrasive character, called Les. He had a sort of glamour about him, because he had been an infantryman

during the war and, unusually, sometimes talked about his experiences. We enjoyed hearing of people blown to smithereens, or cut
in half by machine-gun bullets and were awed to be in the presence
of someone who had actually witnessed these entertainments. Les
still had the wiry physique of the soldier he had been, and was
rumoured still to be handy with his fists when the occasion arose.
Like my own dad, he became eventually a publican. His wife was
Ethel, who had none of the wifely homeliness the name evokes. She
was the only woman I knew who, though grown rather plump,
could feasibly have been called sexy. Once, when we were thirteen
or fourteen, Mickey tied his mother to a kitchen chair. I do not
know why. It must have seemed a good idea at the time. As her legs
were being bound, she looked steadily at me with a stare that was
both appraising and challenging, as she drew suggestively and
deeply on a cigarette. I had no idea what was happening, only that
it was something adult and vaguely filthy. She later left Les, predictably, for a much younger man. There was also a younger
brother – "our Steve" – who occasionally expressed a wish to join
us, but was invariably rebuffed, out of a well-grounded fear that
his discretion could not be relied upon, and, for some years, a collie
dog, called Butch, who was as amiable and uncontrolled as one
might expect of a dog brought up with small boys.

Mickey and I spent a great deal of time just in each other's
company, but would also collect other like-minded souls, who
sometimes joined us, never more than three or four at a time.
There was Royston, who was the only one of us who could have
been called ragged-arsed; on the rare occasions I entered his
house, I recognized a degree of austerity greater than was usual,
even in those days. There were always half-empty milk-bottles
on the table, washing hanging over the chairs and little sign of
comfort anywhere. I do not know where his parents got his name
from; I have only known one other Royston, and he always called
himself "Roy." Perhaps they thought it distinguished. Royston
was recognized to be trouble. From quite early on, he was barred
from our house, having created mayhem at the only birthday
party I was ever permitted to have.

There was Paul, known as "Pill," whose company was much sought after. He lived in a house with a walled garden at the very edge of Bacca's End, right by the canal bridge. I don't think, in truth, that any of us much liked Pill. There was something faintly cruel and sleazy about him. He tortured frogs when he could catch them. Many boys did; others were repelled by the practice, as Mickey and I were. Pill, however, was a little better off than the rest of us, and had some startlingly enviable possessions. He had, for example, an air-rifle, with which he claimed to shoot birds, though I never saw him do so. Better still, he had an old motorcycle: a big, heavy BSA, which was at least thirty years old and had no engine. We would, however, push it to the crown of the canal bridge and freewheel down the gently curving slope and along the towpath, for what seemed like miles, hurtling along at incredible pace, the rider bent over the handlebars, as the rest of us ran behind. Then of course, we had to push it back to the bridge, but that was a small price to pay for such exhilaration. We would do this for hour after hour.

Gerald was a big, rather frightening, boy with thick muscular legs. He lived on the other side of Wednesfield, on the council estate at Ashmore Park, and we did not, therefore, see him very often, nor could we predict when he would appear. He would simply arrive at my house and join in with whatever we were doing or, more frequently, demand that we join some escapade that he was planning. He was the unwitting cause of my learning to swim. He once proposed that we meet at Heath Town Baths. I had boasted, as had he, of my proficiency in the water; in fact, I had never swum without having one foot firmly on the floor. There was no way out. I got to the baths an hour before him and made sure before he arrived that I could do a respectable width. Inevitably, it transpired that he had also lied. He couldn't swim either. Gerald had a tendency to go rather further in mischief than the rest of us. This frightened us, but we valued his equally pronounced tendency to get caught. He acted, rather often, as a lightning conductor for the rest of us. On one occasion, we were throwing pebbles at the bargees on the canal. Gerald led us, and persisted longer than the rest of us. When the bargees gave chase, three of us escaped, but he tripped, was caught and given several solid whacks. He returned dishevelled and weeping, and lashed out at me when I laughed. On another occasion, he cheeked a rather terrifying neighbour of ours: an elderly curmudgeon called Mr. Wright. Mr. Wright was a keen and expert gardener, with a large allotment across the road from his and our house, where he grew vegetables and kept bees. It was understood that to enter this allotment, or otherwise to annoy Mr. Wright, was a crime punishable by death. He was one of that large majority of adults who did not like children and were unamused by the antics of small boys. On one occasion, he was working on his allotment, when Gerald, adapting the words of a popular song, began chanting,

"Don't you rock me, Mr. Wright."

After a few choruses, an explosion occurred in the allotment. The gate burst open, and a large black cloud billowed out. This swiftly resolved itself into the shape of Mr. Wright, bearing down upon us with the kindly intent of a dyspeptic grizzly bear, robbed of its honey. There was no question of flight. There are moments in life when doom inexorably approaches; you cannot dodge; you cannot run away. This was one of them. Gerald found himself seized by a large paw, vigorously shaken, his bones rattled by several vigorous swipes and his backside sorely dented by the imprint of Mr. Wright's size thirteens. He turned to me:

"And as for you. I might 'a knowed yo'd bring all the scum o' the parish round 'ere. I'll tell yerdad!"

This was of course the ultimate sentence. Gerald was seated on the garden wall, softly whining. I regarded him without sympathy. It was alright for him. He didn't have to spend the rest of the day bricking himself.

Mr. Wright's handling of this incident, one may think, smacked slightly of over-reaction. He was in fact a deeply unpleasant man, so much so that he was rumoured once to have been on the Parish Council. He was not a man to provoke. I did so only once, when I ventured into his allotment, and out of curiosity allowed his bees to escape. The ensuing scene was worthy of Hitchcock, as the maddened insects swooped on the village stinging indiscriminately. Or so I have been told. My memory of this is indistinct, but my sister tells me that it happened, and that I confessed. That at least cannot be true. I never, ever confessed. It was against the code. Even when caught in flagrante delicto, with dozens of eye-witnesses, I would always bleat:

"It wor me."

Or, if accompanied:

"It was 'im."

I do, though, remember the sequel, which consisted of Mr. Wright's appearance at our back door and attempting to push past my mother with the announcement that he intended to plant "my toe up 'is arse." He clearly had something of a fixation with toes and small boy's arses. However, my mother was swayed neither by his inexorable logic nor by his feeble attempt at physical violence. If there was one thing she was sure of, it was that the infliction of trauma upon her children's rears would remain securely within the family. A battle ensued, of which the outcome was never in doubt. The enemy retreated. Any relief or gratitude I might have felt, however, was dispelled by the pronouncing of the inevitable sentence:

"Ah'tell Yerdad when 'e comes 'ome."

Mr. Wright had a son Thomas, large like himself and some four years older than me. He was courteous and well-spoken, both of which qualities instantly identified him as a potential victim. He was rarely to be seen. When I did see him, I attacked him. Usually, he would cry, but none of these assaults led to consequences.

I assume that either Thomas did not rat on me, or that his father was embarrassed to complain on behalf of a son twice as large as his attacker. I do not think my assaults were especially vindictive. In our approach to fighting, we were like young animals. If we were not otherwise engaged, we fought.

There was also, quite regularly, Ian, who lived closer to me than any of my other friends. Ian was whiplash-thin, fair-haired and physically by far the most competent and adventurous of all my friends. I felt some unease in his company, because I often found my courage tested by a challenge to climb a tree, or shin up a half-completed building. In those days, the Black Country was undergoing something of an economic recovery after the depression, the war and the years of postwar austerity. There were many, many building sites, and an equal number of old buildings in various states of demolition. Health and safety, particularly that of small boys, was not then the obsession it has since become. Access to building sites was easy, and there were few watchmen to scare us off after work or at the weekends. Ian could climb scaffolding with the ease and grace of an Orang-Utan swinging through the jungles of Borneo or Sarawak. Mickey and I were less adept, and a good deal less brave. I remember in particular one day when Ian tightrope walked across a plank stretched between the upper storeys of two half-complete houses and dared us to follow. We, needless to say, adopted the usual stratagem of saying that we had already done it, the previous day, when no one had been looking.

Ian invented the canal bridge test. This entailed leaping from the parapet of an upward-sloping stone bridge, the winner being the one who jumped from the highest point onto a small patch of scruffy grass below. It was vital to roll forward immediately on landing, otherwise you fell back and cracked your head against the stone. I once concussed myself doing this, sufficiently severely to spend twenty-four hours in hospital. Mickey, showing a presence of mind that was far from characteristic of him, explained to my mother that I had fallen while playing football. It added greatly to the amenity of this game – the leaping, not the football

– that the patch of grass on which we landed and rolled over was a favourite stopping place beside the canal for dogs out for the evening walkies.

"Ave yo bin rollin in bloody dog-shit?"

Our outraged mothers would howl, when we arrived home reeking. This was of course before the invention of the "poop-scoop." Now, no dog-walker feels properly equipped unless he is clutching a bag full of steaming ordure in his eager grasp.

Dogs were a significant part of our lives, though until I was about ten, when Butch arrived and we ourselves engaged the services of a short lived Corgi called Sandy, none of us kept one. It was in those days the custom to allow dogs to roam wild. Some took full advantage of this liberty to lead lives even more lawless than ours, chasing after us at will, puncturing our plastic footballs, biting if we interfered with them, or at least threatening to do so. There was one which lived around the corner from us: small, old, grey and ratlike. We were justly afraid of its propensity to attack on sight.

When I look back, it is astonishing to recollect how confined our lives were. We knew by sight boys from other schools and from other years in our own school, but we rarely associated with them. When we did so, the contact usually had an element of violence or abuse. A slightly younger boy called Jonathan lived a few doors up the street. His name was considered ample justification for punching his head, and we did so frequently. Often, this pro-voked complaint, and at least once the pronouncing of the awful sentence:

"yo wait till Yerdad comes 'ome."

I once subjected him to yet further humiliation by urging my sister to beat him up, too, which she gladly did. This was uncommon: girls usually practised violence only on each other, apart from a notorious psychopath called, ominously, Gaynor, who delivered newspapers, and was known to punch heads indiscriminately, on sight.

There was also a child called Julian, a name even more meet for penalty. He was known, moreover, to be a cut above; he went to a school with a uniform that consisted of a grey blazer and flannels. However, he had an older brother, and rarely went out except in convoy. I also remember, rather painfully, a short, thickset boy who was known, universally, as "Wicked." I once punched him in an altercation at the fish-shop door. Mickey had, I think, knocked his bag of chips to the floor. "Wicked" grabbed both my hands and started to kick both my shins, hard, with metal-tipped boots. The pain was excruciating. I limped tearfully away. From then on, Wicked was immune from further assault.

Our lives were confined socially and geographically. We rarely went beyond The Park, Bacca's End, the Canal Towpath or my Grandparents' house, about a mile away. For years, the walk to my Grandparents' offered the prospect of adventure, because it led through what had been scruffy wasteland, but had become the site of the new Wednesfield Council Offices in what was christened "Alfred Squire Road." Alfred Squire was, I think, a coal merchant whom democracy, in a moment of aberration, had elevated to the Council.

Our lives were also regulated by the Seasons. I do not simply mean the relatively trivial matters determined by the position of our bit of the Earth's surface in relation to the sun. We took little notice of the passage of summer, via autumn, into winter, which was marked for us largely by the occasional parental injunction (half-hearted and usually ignored) to "put yer bloody coat on." The transition from football to cricket and vice-versa was far more important to us, and rigorously observed. It helped that the seasons were more distinct then. The Cup Final was held on the first Saturday in May, the league season having ended a couple of weeks before that; cricket began in the last week of April. No self-respecting child ever played either game out of season. I remember once a few of us attempting a game of cricket after the end of the school summer holidays. It felt wrong; we attracted a small and silently disapproving group of spectators, as though we had ventured outside wearing our sisters' dresses. We soon gave up. Other activities similarly waxed and waned with the seasons, as though the rhythm of our lives had been determined by the Book of Ecclesiastes. There was a season for marbles, a season for jacks, a season for conkers, and of course a glorious few weeks in each year when fireworks could be brought and used as weapons of mass terror.

The conduct of our games was, similarly, highly regulated – but the regulation was entirely a matter of shared understanding. We never, for example, played on a marked pitch, either for cricket or football, but there was rarely any dispute as to whether a ball was "in" or "out" or "over", or had gone for four or six, and in cricket leg-before decisions were arrived at, sometimes following fierce debate, by a consensus between batsman and bowler not usually evident in more elevated manifestations of the sport. Adjudication in football was simplified by the fact that there were no off-sides, and no fouls other than handball. There were also in general no tactics: basically, we all pursued the ball and dribbled greedily until someone took it from us. The best player was a doleful-looking boy called Roger who had the advantage of being extremely quick. Once in possession, unless instantly tripped, he could not be caught. He could be thwarted only by the goalkeeper, or by a concerted shout of "over the bar!" if his shot rose more than four feet from the ground. Generally, though, our games were a formless melee.

That is not to say, though, that they were without moments when they felt much as sport must feel to those rare beings who can play it well. I still remember the unique pleasure gained from a skilful run, followed by a crisp shot, or, in cricket, from a correctly timed stroke, hit in the "meat" of the bat. Sport is one of the most elitist of activities, but almost anyone can from time to time experience a moment that is like any moment in the life of a Sobers or a Tom Finney. I loved sport, especially football, to a degree that now, when I have lost almost any interest whatever in football, I find it hard to imagine.

Once, when we were about twelve, Mickey and I decided to ride our bikes to Bridgnorth. This is a pretty little place about twelve miles from Wolverhampton. It has an old town on a hill, which can be reached by a funicular railway. Those who do not know it will imagine from this description that it is a kind of Midlands equivalent of Zermatt. Not so, in fact, but Mickey had described the hill outside Bridgnorth, the Hermitage, as a sort of steeper version of the Matterhorn. I was curious to see this, so off we went, early one Saturday morning. It was easily the furthest either of us had been unaccompanied by an adult to that point. Needless to say, we did not inform our parents of our intentions. The journey there was uneventful, past the ivy-clad walls of Wolverhampton Grammar School and the Edwardian villas on the Compton Road, but we soon discovered that 12 miles on a bicycle is quite a long way to those unaccustomed to the distance.

The Hermitage is not quite as formidable as legend represented it, but it was nonetheless thrilling to freewheel down it to the River Severn, past what seemed to us cliffs of red sandstone. There, by the river, we rested in sight of the old brick houses, some of them unprecedentedly grand, piled high on the opposite bank, rising to the High Town. We somehow sensed that this was a place both older and posher than anything we usually saw in Wednesfield. For a time, we lay exhausted in the grass, and I remember pressing my face to the ground and realizing that, far from being merely and dully green, the grass was compounded of a thousand bright lights where the sun spread through it. I doubt if Mickey felt the same, for I woke from my reverie to see him skipping flat stones over the slow moving surface of the Severn.

"Ow many yo done?" I asked, meaning how many times had he caused a stone to deflect from the surface of the water.

"Twenty three," he improbably replied.

"I bet yo ay. Come on, let's see oo can do the most."

For some reason, perhaps because I had gripped my handlebars so tightly as I freewheeled down the Hermitage, my wrist had no flexibility that day. Normally, I beat Mickey easily in this contest of skill. Today, try as I might, I could achieve no more than three leaps, and the majority of my efforts sank immediately and ingloriously on first contact with the river.

"Yo're fuckin useless, Singo," he cackled triumphantly. We had just gone to secondary school, the immediate, and in his case almost the only, effect of which had been to enlarge our vocabulary, introducing us to words whose meaning we could define imprecisely if at all, but which we instinctively guessed, would not translate to the parental home. Without apparent effort, he flicked an "eighter" over the surface, startling a somnolent duck. As he turned contemptuously away, I bent to gather a clod to throw at the back of his oblivious neck – a part of his anatomy he liked, for some reason, to refer to as "the chivvy." A lump of muddy earth down his chivvy struck me as just the thing to restore the balance of a relationship that had just gone, so far as I was concerned, seriously out of kilter. Grasping a tuft of grass, I heaved mightily. The earth resisted for a time, like the stone in which the sword Excalibur sat, then at last it gave way, with an appalling and destabilizing suddenness.

There were many moments in my young life when I clearly saw the rapid onrush of approaching doom – those moments, for example, when I had just hit a stone, and was in the act of catapulting over the handlebars of my bicycle. A strange lucidity, a peculiar detachment takes over; I suppose other people feel this, too. You think to yourself:

"In a second, this will really, really hurt."

But for that instant, it is as though you were outside yourself and merely observing. So it was with me, as I teetered on the bank of the Severn. I knew with a dreadful certainty that my balance was past the point of recovery, yet there was, for a minuscule fraction of a second, an ominous pause before I actually fell. There I was, completely unobserved by anyone else, and yet a being on the very edge of catastrophe. Silently, I fell. Only when I hit the water, did the splash alert people to my fate. I was not completely immersed. I stood, in water up to my thighs, conscious of the grinning faces on the river bank, among them that of my erstwhile friend. I hauled myself out.

"Yo alright, Singo?"

"Course! Bin for a fuckin' swim, ay I?"

With that, and with such dignity as I could muster, I picked up my bike and set off on the long ride home, not waiting for Mickey.

"Eh, wait for me. I dow know the way 'ome."

And so we set off, myself disconsolate and humiliated, Mickey irritated by the abrupt termination of his day out. We spoke little on the way back.

As we reached the outskirts of Wolverhampton, we both became tired and began to wobble. I was immediately behind Mickey, when my front wheel collided, quite gently, with his rear one. He was able, by sticking out his leg, to prevent himself from falling. My bicycle clipped the kerb, enabling me for the second time that day to appreciate the persuasive power of Sir Isaac Newton's best known invention. It would be an exaggeration to say that I "sailed," or "hurtled" from my seat. My dive over the handlebars of my bicycle more strongly resembled the trajectory of a falling brick than the dive of a swallow. Nevertheless I flatter myself that I achieved, over a short flightpath, a considerable inertia. Once more, I had the pleasure of internally reflecting:

"This is going to bloody hurt,"

Followed by the further pleasure of being proved entirely correct. There may be areas of England where road are bordered by areas of softly yielding savannah, green carpets, soft as thistledown, into which a falling body can sink and feel only a gentle and gracious embrace. This is not, however, the case with the roads around Wolverhampton; they offer no inducement to the would-be diver. They are bordered with pavements, hard, grey and unyielding. It was onto one of these that I now descended.

I had been right. It bloody hurt. I started to cry, as a couple, seeing me fall stopped their car, wound down the passenger side window, and called out:

"You okay, son."

"Yeah, " I lied, out of a juvenile conviction that, however bad things were, adult intervention would make them infinitely worse. Above all, as with most of the things that happened to me, my first instinct was to make as sure as I could that my Dad would not find out. It would be the perfect ending to a perfect day to get home and hear my mother say,

"Yo wait till yerdad gets 'ome."

I rose to my feet, unsteadily conscious of grazed hands, knees and elbows, but of something else, too, something more serious. My right wrist felt even sorer than the rest of me. I tried to lift my bicycle, and squealed in pain. It was obvious that riding was out of the question.

There are moments so dire that even a small boy will evince some concern.

"Yo ok, Singo?" asked Mickey, somewhat idiotically, since it must have been spectacularly obvious that I was not ok.

73

"Dow think I can ride me bike," I replied with all the considerable self-pity of which I am capable. At this point, Mickey proved himself a true friend. He grasped both bikes, and so we walked home, with him wheeling the two cycles. We must have walked six miles, and it took several hours, trudging along the Bridgnorth road on a hot day. It did not occur to either of us to ask for help, though it would surely have been given. In extremis, whenever things went wrong, our first concern was always to conceal the facts from adults. So it was then. When eventually I got home (Mickey having immediately scarpered for fear of reprisals), I said nothing at first, but was evidently in pain:

"What's up wi' yer?" asked my mother.

"Nothin'"

"Doh gi me that. Yo ay cryin' for nothin'. What's up wi' yer arm?

"I fell off mi' bike an 'urt it.'

"Oh David, yo doh arf worry me! Let's 'ave a look. Oh bloody 'el. Look 'ere Al. Look what 'e's done. 'is wrist's all swollen."

My mother was weeping at this point. As she hugged me, I registered the fact that she smelled slightly of chip fat. This was no surprise. Nor was it a surprise that, for all its inadequacies and despite the tensions then just beginning as we moved out of early childhood, home was still an essentially comforting place, one to which a tangible hurt could be brought and find a readiness to heal. I was, of course, immediately dispatched to the hospital, where the damage was found to be sufficiently severe to require manipulation under a general anaesthetic. My broken wrist was then encased in a plaster, which served me well as a club for the ensuing six weeks.

Our lives as small boys seem to me to have been extraordinarily carefree and immune from consequences. We were not William and the Outlaws, and we knew no one in that social class, but we behaved with comparable lawlessness, and no fear of repercussions beyond the occasional smacking. No one depicted us as juvenile delinquents, and if it was generally recognized that my friends and I were dirty, disorderly, mischievous and anarchic, there was a consensus that not much else was to be expected. We were, after all, boys. I had the dubious advantage, when I was very small, of being rather angelic in appearance, with large blue eyes, which could look soulful when I was hungry or planning mischief, and golden curly hair, a ringlet of which was kept by my mother throughout her life. I would sometimes, though only ever inadvertently, arrive in the house when my mother was talking to her friends. My arrival, usually with a holster strapped around my waist and a bow across my shoulders, would always occasion some comment:

"Oo 'ay e got lovely 'air!"

Or

"E 'ay 'alf grown!"

Once, my Aunt Janey was there, and said, to my bewilderment:

"E'll break some 'earts, 'e will."

Why, I wondered, should I want to do that, and how did one go about it. It was the sort of thing adults said from time to time. It corresponded to no reality with which one was familiar, and it was best simply to ignore it.

My Aunt Janey probably knew something about broken hearts. She was my grandmother's sister and styled herself Miss Jane Skitt. However, she was in fact a widow. Her husband, who had been depressive, had drowned himself in the Wednesfield and Bentley canal many years before. Janey had lived alone ever since in uncomplaining poverty in a mid-nineteenth-century terraced house with an outside lavatory and a well in the yard. That was by then closed off, but had been the only source of water for several families. At the time, I thought it an exciting concept and a privilege to draw one's water from an actual well.

Janey's house was the only one in the family, other than Florrie's, that could be called or aspired to be spotlessly clean. Despite this, it smelled slightly of damp, overboiled cabbage and general lack of ventilation. The sitting room was the smallest I knew. The furniture was black and somewhat unyielding. There was a small collection of pretty glass, a table with a white lace top and an aspidistra in a green pot on it. There was a large, black bible and various religious pictures on the wall, for Janey was, uncharacteristically for our family, known to be devout. There were photographs of men with moustaches and one of Janey herself as a younger woman, looking much as she still did in her seventies. Best of all, there was a harmonium, with which I was fascinated. I knew that it could produce music, without having actually to be played and was anxious to witness this – for me – slightly fabulous process. I once asked my Grandad, who always took me to Janey's – she lived a busride away in Willenhall in Peel street; – whether my Aunty could be persuaded to let me have a go on it.

"No lad," he replied, "Ah dow think she likes ter 'ear it no more."

I now assume that the harmonium had belonged to her husband, and that it had been kept out of piety, but that to play it would bring back too many memories.

My sister Pauline recently showed me a picture of Janey as a young woman. She is holding my Auntie Florrie, who must then have been about three. That places the photograph in about 1907. Janey was already then a widow, and is dressed in black, in full Edwardian costume, with bodice , a high neck and a wasp waist. She looks elegant, beautiful and maternal. It appears that she was much concerned by my grandmother's lack of any discernible instinct for mothering, and spent as much of her time with the children as she was allowed to and gave them such experience of feminine tenderness as they received.

I liked going to my Aunt Janey's. Despite her sadness, there was a sparkle about her, with her wire spectacles and hair tied back in a tight bun, covered with a net. She had few visitors, was always glad to see us and produced tea and Nice biscuits. She lived long enough for her continued survival to become a matter for some surprise. For the last few years of her life, she moved into an old person's bungalow not far from Florrie, who looked after her, as best she could, with help from Hazel and my mother, until my father forbade her to go.

There is a story to this, that reflects little credit on the institution of the family. In her last years, Aunt Janey became blind. She was also in the habit of keeping such money as she possessed hidden in the house. The money disappeared, as did her glass and her little bits of china and glass. She was not much exercised about this; she no longer had any need for money, and she could no longer see the knick-knacks. She had relatives, whom we barely knew, who, so the story goes, robbed her. My father, regarding this as the ultimate disgrace, was afraid my mother would be blamed. If this is true, Janey deserved a good deal better. I prefer to think that it may not be true, though my sister assures me that it is. Elderly people often become confused about their possessions; they give them away and forget they have done so, and it is all too easy for a blind person to break a piece of glass or porcelain, clear it away, and forget that it has happened – or to conceal it on inquiry.

Visits to relatives, though, were rare. For the most part, like my friends, when I was not at school, I was left to my own devices. Like other aspects of our play, our skulduggery was regulated by a set of observances of unknown origin. We would, for example, decide that our day was to be devoted to "green apple." This consisted of knocking on doors and running away, leaving the intensely irritated adult within to emerge and glare furiously around. To gain the maximum benefit from this, it was necessary to appoint a viewing station from which to watch the enraged inmate appear. Unfortunately, we frequently did this ineptly, so that we ourselves were visible. The result was inevitable:

"Ah'll tell yower Mom about you, David Singleton."

This struck a chill, but at the age of ten, teatime is a lifetime away. An extra refinement of green apple was, as already mentioned, the posting of a ready lit banger. Equally satisfying, and permissible under the rules of green apple was the insertion of the said banger into an empty milk-bottle standing on the doorstep. Further excitement was added on the occasions when the bottle was adjacent to a sleeping dog or cat. There was no prospect of doing serious harm – we all liked dogs, and treated cats with a respect proportionate to their readiness to employ weapons in their own defence – since the explosion was not powerful enough to burst the bottle; but it sounded like a gunburst and inevitably led to panicked flight on the part of the animal, rudely woken from some carnivorous dream.

Annoying cats was in general regarded as legitimate sport, partly because cats are easily annoyed and partly because their attitude to small boys is a peculiarly obnoxious compound of wariness, aggression and disdain. The cat we had at home could not really be described as a "pet". He would use the house, with not the least gratitude, and sleep malodorously (he was a full tom) on the furniture, departing when he thought it was time for a night of sex, slaughter and larceny. If I sat by him, he would open a baleful eye, and growl, softly and menacingly. If I attempted to touch him, the growl would turn into a hiss.

We all employed, as one of our favourite weapons, pea-shooters – in the season, of course. From, I think, May onwards, we would spend a high proportion of our by no means lavish pocket money on ammunition for pea-shooters. This was a sort of dried pea, sold by the shop which purveyed fishing tackle and bait, such as maggots, known to us as "grey farters." From a range up to about 15 yards, these could hit hard enough to sting, and certainly hard enough to prompt a sleeping cat into resentful escape. Pill was rumoured to have shot and killed a cat with his .22 airgun, but I do not think this was true. Because he lived on the edges of the wilderness that was Bacca's End, he was a person about whom legends tended to collect; naturally, he did nothing to deny them. The killing of a cat, however, would have been impossible for the rest of us in reality to stomach. We intended, not to maim or kill, but to irritate, and in this we succeeded.

Our other game, more boasted of than indulged in, was "red apple." This involved breaking a window with a carefully aimed pebble. Ian once did this when the occupant of the house was looking through the said window – an act of dangerous bravado, which brought on him predictably painful consequences. We saw little of him in the ensuing months. The rest of us took a similarly sensuous pleasure in the tinkle of broken glass, but tended to confine our endeavours to buildings we knew to be deserted. Thus, we took a heavy toll on old factories at weekends, though on occasions these proved not to be unoccupied, and we would find ourselves chased – though happily never caught, or identified, by irate workmen.

Theft was not a regular part of our repertoire, but nor was it something to which we had any particular moral exception. Any parent who believes that his or her children has not on occasion indulged in a little larceny has, in my view, forgotten their own childhood. I recall a glorious day spent on Wolverhampton Low Level Station – not normally remarkable for luxe, calme et volupte when one of us, I think Royston, discovered that the vending machine for Nestle's chocolate could be held open so that, for the cost of one sixpence, the entire machine could be emptied. Between three of us, we ate so much chocolate that I think none us has touched Nestle's chocolate since. Gerald once extended these activities into actual shoplifting, stealing from the sweets counter in Woolworths. To general contempt, I wimped out on this, as did Mickey. It was simply too dangerous.

We did not, none of us did, regard the unauthorized taking of growing things as theft; more of a duty, so that we took even such things as raspberries, little though we cared for them. "Scrumping" for apples and pears was a serious occupation for the autumn. We had our favourite targets, chosen more for the calculated daring needed for success than for the quality of the loot. One such was a big house by the canal. It had a high mesh fence, leaving about four feet of shrubbery before the ground fell away into the canal. In order to get to the apple trees, it was necessary to drop from the canal bridge into the shrubbery, itself fraught with danger, as the ground was uneven and could easily precipitate a necessary, but unsought, bath. Then, you had to sneak along the shrubbery to a place where the fence was slightly loose at the bottom and could be lifted just enough for a small boy to crawl under. It was vital to remain unobserved, because the only means of escape was to climb back up the bridge at its junction with the meshing fence: a slow process, even when unencumbered by stolen fruit.

Inevitably, one day we were caught. Mickey and I were aloft in an apple tree, when its owner appeared at the bottom. Disappointingly, he threatened no revenge:

"Oi, yoh little buggers. Doh yow get climbing my trees. If yoh want the apples, yoh can 'ave them. I cor stand the bloody things."

Naturally, his property lost all attraction for us from that day on. Deprived of its essential attraction, danger, it became, not a fortress to be penetrated, but just another rather large and boring house.

The canal at that point marked, for us, the end of the village. The road bore right immediately after the bridge, and the council, in its constant concern for the entertainment of small boys, placed a public lavatory there sometime in the late 50's. It may still be there. The physical needs of Black Country folk are unlikely to have changed much. I wonder if small boys still stand outside the locked cubicles chanting,

"We know what you're up to."

Or

"That was a real old stinker. Give us another one, do."

Or if they fire grey farters – at the correct season – over the tops of the doors onto the sufferer beneath.

Across the road, there was, and surely still is, The Dog and Partridge Pub, reputed to be five hundred years old and to be the oldest building in Wednesfield. As though to lend substance to these claims, there were black rails outside, claimed to be for tethering horses. It was impressed upon us that, whatever other crimes we committed, we must not touch those rails. Apparently they were like the ravens in the Tower. Without those rails, the rich and verdant realm that was Wednesfield would pass mournfully into history. Those black, rather dull, structures therefore fascinated us. There was in truth little one could do with them. They were too low to swing on, too narrow to tightrope walk across, too high to be a challenge for limbo dancing. All you could really do, presumably like the horses of yesteryear, was hang around, rather glumly. Even that, however, was sufficient to invite the satisfaction of adult disapproval and the thrill of being chased away. It could have been disheartening to have spent so much of one's first twelve years being told to "bugger off"; it could have damaged one's self-esteem, had it been invented then. Somehow, it just felt right; it fitted the concept one had of oneself as essentially an outlaw.

The canal – universally known as the "cut" – had of course a magnetism for us. Canals still had a practical purpose in the Black Country in those days. Great horses still pulled barges laden with coal along them, not least to my father's works, leaving huge steaming turds of enviable proportions on the narrow towpaths. The bargees were heroic figures, muscular, sweaty men, inconceivably filthy and both in that respect and in the vigour of their incessant cursing, role models (had we known the concept) to us all. They also occasionally left huge steaming turds on the towpath. They were not, however, friends: too many had no doubt received a pebble behind the ear, hurled by small boys from a canal bridge. It was known that to be caught by a bargee was to court a particularly horrible death.

Improbable as it seems, men would sit at weekends patiently fishing in those coal-black, drowned-cat-rich waters, hour after hour with no prospect of any catch more exotic or more edible than the humble roach or gudgeon. Such, it may be, are the lengths to which men will go to escape the blessings of female companionship. It was our particular joy to send a pebble into the water immediately by a fisherman, thereby disturbing the immense pike that, in his imagination, was at that very moment about to nibble on the proffered maggot. We ourselves, without of course a licence, would occasionally sit with becoming solemnity, imitating our elders. Ian had the gear, and Mickey soon acquired it: rod and line, basket and reel: the reels were especially prestigious, as complex as the Large Hadron Collider, the more complicated the better. In the end, I acquired Mickey's rod and reel, exchanging my bike for it. This provoked fury at home, and a rapid annulment of the deal through parental negotiation. In truth, I never much liked fishing, and was glad that the vogue for it lasted perhaps no more than two years. I hated pushing the maggots onto the hook, and watching squashy stuff come out of them. Then, too, on the mercifully infrequent occasions when a fish was caught, I found barbaric the process of extracting the hook from its lip, and pointless the practice of securing it in a keepnet till it was time to go home, when there was nothing more to be done with it than let it go. If I learned a lesson from this about the ugliness of gratuitous cruelty, it was a salutary one. I am not sure it was worth all those torn piscine lips to teach me what I should have known anyway.

At one time or another, we all fell in the canal, none more gloriously than Gerald. We found a tin bath, and persuaded him that it was seaworthy. He barely fitted into it, for he was a big lad, but into it, one way or another, he got. He may have felt a little like Captain Bligh receiving the good wishes of Mr.Christian and his friends as he left his native shore, for we had as little thought of helping him, as we pushed the tin bath away. For a moment, several moments, it achieved an improbable, obviously temporary, stability. It floated, with Gerald in it, just about. Then, inch by inch, it began to settle in the water; then the water began to lap over what we might in our imagination have called its gunwales. Gerald looked at us with an utterly hapless expression, as we hooted with laughter on the towpath. How we laughed! We laughed till our ribs hurt and we thought our lungs would burst. I cannot say exactly how Gerald recovered terra firma, for there was a point at which, fearing a violent reaction, we felt it politic to escape. He was at school the next day, but it was some weeks before he spoke to us.

It would be hard to decide what was the most lawless thing we ever did. We once set fire, not wholly deliberately, to an outhouse; Pill once crapped in the changing-room at Heath Town baths, and left a large brown turd for the next occupant of the cubicle to discover. Secretly, the rest of us found that rather disgusting, and we saw little of Pill subsequently. The glamour of his possessions was not, in the final analysis, enough to compensate for the fact that his boundaries were staked out somewhat further into criminality than those of the rest of us.

Mickey and I were only once apprehended by the police: for no worse a crime than leaning on a paling fence outside a house in process of construction. Admittedly, we were leaning quite hard, and had succeeded in moving the fence some degrees out of the vertical. We saw the uniformed policemen some distance away, and moved smartly off – not running, because to run would have been to put oneself definitively beyond the law. We simply walked much more quickly than usual, rounded several corners and looked back. There was the policeman, precisely the same distance away.

"E ay after us, is 'e?" asked Mickey.

"I doh know."

And so we moved off again, again rounding corners, pausing once more. There he was again, menacing in his relentless lack of hurry. There could be no doubt that he was in pursuit of us; no doubt either that he was in no hurry, certain of his quarry. Helplessly we looked at each other; neither of us could come up with an escape plan. Again, we set off, and again. Every time we looked back, the policeman was there. Now I knew how the wrongdoer felt when pursued by the Canadian Mounties, who always got their man. After what felt like many hours, we were in reach of my home.

"Run for it when we get round the corner," I said tearfully.

Run we did, as we had never run before. Around the corner, through the gate, along the drive and into the scullery, hoping to have escaped.

For some time, we thought we had done it. Then we heard a heavy, authoritative thump on the door. If we could have wished a heart attack on ourselves at that moment we would have done it.

"What is it?" asked my mother.

"Like a word about yower lad," said the constable.

Things could not be worse. As always, though, when things cannot get any worse, they promptly did.

"OO's that?" called a masculine voice. My Dad was home!

"It's the police."

"It ay, is it? What's our bloody David been up to now?"

In calmer times, I would have been stung by the manifest unfairness of this. Here I was being convicted, not merely without evidence, but even without identification of the crime of which I was accused. However, it was not the unfairness of it all that weighed upon me at that moment, but the inevitability of punishment.

My parents were law-abiding people. For a policeman to call at the house with a complaint was a disgrace. There was to be no argument. If the police said I was guilty, I was. That was all there was to it. The interview with the law was brief. The constable explained what had happened; phrases like "malicious damage" were audible, as I sized up the odds of sidling through the half-inch wide hole in the well-cover to accept a welcome and merciful death by drowning. Finally, he asked to see me:

"Nah then, lad," he began, "what yoh was doin' is a crime. Ah could put yoh in jail for it, but I shar. Ah'm gonna let yerdad deal wi' it instead."

"No!" I thought "Put me in jail. For years. Decades! Until medad's got too old and weak to give me the hiding of a lifetime, which was surely coming.

It did, but not immediately. I was told to wait, while my Dad escorted Mickey back to his home, to ensure that he too received the appropriate and invariable punishment. It was small consolation to me later, as I stood with tears pouring down my cheeks and my backside tingling to know that my best friend had suffered, or was suffering the same fate, though there is always a little compensatory pleasure in the reflection that, whatever one is suffering oneself, one's friends are suffering equally. My father preceded the inevitable beating with a series of remarks on the theme of disgracing the family. I wish I could say that these hurt more, but they did not. I was a good deal more concerned about the pain in my arse than the condition of my soul.

Winter, naturally enough, provided more opportunities for dubious adventure. We had, of course, none of the winter gear that is taken for granted now: an extra cardigan, a balaclava and woollen gloves were the best we could hope for. The last of these could be worse than useless: cold, wet and bedraggled after half an hour's snowballing or sledging. There were no bright red toboggans to be bought in the shops then, or if there were we did not see them, but someone's dad could always be prevailed upon to make a sleigh, improvised out of the bits of spare wood everyone had in those days, retained just in case it might come in handy. Above all, we had snow. This is one of the areas in which memory is most likely to be deceptive, but my recollection is that we had snow year after year. Doubtless, this was not really the case, but it seems it in retrospect, merely because those are the winters one remembers.

We also had fog: deep, luscious fog, as thick as beef stew: fog you could taste, and roll on your tongue; fog that stayed for days on your clothes; fog in which you could see nothing and, better still, be seen by no one; fog in which green apple and red apple offered new opportunities, ruthlessly exploited, for scot-free skulduggery. At least once in every winter, usually more than once, a classic coal-fire-thickened fog would bring all traffic to a halt. School would close blissfully early. Of course, there was no nonsense about parental collection. The children were simply tipped out and left to grope their way home. We expected nothing else.

Fog, snow and ice! What could be better? We were impervious to cold and, besides, it was no warmer in than out, and our parents were no more anxious for our company in the dark days of winter than in spring or summer. Our lives, outside school, were still lived in the open air, even when it was scarcely breathable. We made slides, always on pavements, so that we had the vicarious pleasure of seeing adults venture unsuspecting onto them and fall, crashing to the ground. Long, glistening, treacherous slides, down which we hurled ourselves at full tilt, occasionally retaining balance, more often ending on our backsides. There was rivalry between teams of slidemakers, which often involved sabotage. A small scattering of ashes, strategically placed, could wreck a slide, and bring an unsuspecting slider crashing to a halt. We sledged, on our improvised wooden boards, down the steep white slag-heaps of Bacca's End, taking turns and competing as to who could travel furthest, the air whipping our faces a furious red. And we threw snowballs.

They say that the Inuit peoples of the far North have many different words for snow. If I had known this as a small boy, I would have thought it completely natural and unsurprising. We were connoisseurs of snow. We could tell, even as it fell, whether it would compact into a usable missile; best was the part frozen snow that, moulded in the hands, could become a ball of ice that would do service as a cannonball. These we reserved for serious snowball fights between rival gangs of boys, when we were out to hurt, and not merely surprise. For girls, we reserved more friable snow that would break on contact and, if well-aimed would deposit snow fragments down the back of the neck. We snowballed the girls mainly to clear them from the school playground so that serious hostilities could commence. Wisely, the teachers did not venture outside.

We used the softer snow also for our less frequent attacks on adults. One Sunday morning, Mickey and I were playing in the snow, when a man neither of us knew went past. Having, a well-constructed snowball in his hand, Mickey naturally let him have it. Mickey was not normally accurate in his throws; he held his own through rapidity of fire, rather than specificity of aim. On this day, however, the Gods were with him. The snowball screeched through the air like a heat-seeking missile and disintegrated on the back of the man's head, depositing snow down his open collar.

"Yo little buggers!" he yapped, perceptively.

We ran for it, Mickey gloating:

"Right down 'is chivvy. Right down the back of 'is chivvy. Did yer see that chuck, Singo, right down 'is chivvy!"

I got the general drift. Mickey's triumphs were infrequent. He was not the boy to allow one to pass without due celebration.

Sundays meant Sunday lunch, for which one's presence was required. The radio was always on, as the morning declined into lunchtime. There was "Round the Horne," which was incomprehensible. Surely there could be no one really called J.Peasmole Gruntfuttock, and if there were, why did he speak so strangely. At some point in each programme, two ladylike voices would greet each other:

"Hello Rodney"

"Hello Charles"

Mystified, I once asked my mother,

"Why do they talk like that?"

"They'm cissies," she mysteriously replied.

It still astonishes me that at a time when homosexuality was both illegal and not officially admitted to exist (a difficult double act to bring off), the BBC should have allowed Kenneth Williams and Hugh Paddick to camp it up so outrageously and brilliantly. It was, of course, all lost on me. I preferred Take it from Here, because it featured "The Glums," a lugubrious couple not unlike many of the people I saw about me day to day. Worse, there was "Family Favourites," patronizingly presented by Jean Metcalf and Cliff Michelmore, the main point of which appeared to be to illustrate the predictably limited musical tastes of Her Majesty's Forces abroad. There were, it is true, "classical" bon-bons: Kathleen Ferrier singing "Che faro senza Eurydice," or Kenneth MacKellar making a decent fist of "ombra mai fu," but these were lost in the floodtide of "mud, mud, glorious mud," "the laughing police-man" and "Daddy wouldn't buy me a bow-wow." The message to our brave boys overseas appeared to be that, however far you fled, British humour would find you in the end.

I cannot in all honesty say that these thoughts occurred to me at the time. While various songsters trilled away in the background, I read. I had a large number of those red-bound children's classics that were so familiar a part of the 50s childhood; some were written for children, others most definitely not. I first encountered the Brontes between those postbox covers. It may have been Lorna Doone I was reading. I read it several times, enraptured by the heroism of John Ridd and by the heroine who was, as expected of nineteenth century heroines, beautiful, and otherwise a cipher. As I was reading, my father came in:

"What yo' bin doin' today, David?"

"Readin?"

He sat down beside me on the couch.

"What yo' readin'?"

"Lorna Doone."

"Yeah, ah've read that. Good, ay it? Excitin'.

This was, by this time, rare. I was by now about twelve, and my father had become often distant to me. He occasionally let me "help" him when he was fiddling with the car, which was almost every day, but his manner was often short, and his main impact on my life sometimes seemed to be to administer the sanctions demanded by my mother.

"Ave yo done anythin' else, today?"

"Bin outside, playin' in the snow, with Mickey."

"Oh ar? Bin throwin' snowballs?'

"No dad." By now, my instinct for danger was fully aroused.

"Why is it then that this bloke said 'e went past yo two in the street, and one of yer chucked a bloody snowball down the back of his neck?" This said on a tone of rising anger.

"Twor me. It was Mickey."

"I dow care who it was. Yo was there, and up to mischief as usual. Ah dow like people comin' up and complainin' about my kid. Now, yer can go off to yer room and stay there till I say yo can come down."

This was said in a tone of quiet self-satisfaction that hurt more than any tirade, any beating.

Mostly, then, as children we made our own entertainment and incurred our own punishments. There were occasional organized events, which of course we did what we could to subvert. Our primary school, for example, once dragooned us into a choral competition. We were rehearsed for this by the Headmaster for months, and in fact we won first prize. The competition was held in the somewhat second-rate splendour of the Wolverhampton Civic Hall, which naturally none of us had entered before. During the competition itself, perhaps somewhat in awe of the surroundings, we behaved reasonably well. However, as a special treat, we were allowed, nay compelled, to remain in the audience to hear the Headmaster's own choir participate in the adult competition. We watched from a high balcony as these, to us, improbably elderly men in dull suits began to sing. I have no idea what they sang. They began on a low tone, as though humming. As the first note sounded, one of us, I cannot say who, began to laugh; by the second note we were all struggling not to laugh; by the third, we had given up the struggle. Our class teacher intervened:

"Out!" he whispered savagely, holding open a heavy swing door.

Out we staggered, holding our sides. Mickey and I rolled on the red baize carpet outside, laughing helplessly. Royston went one better. He rolled down the thickly carpeted stairway, and was still laughing as he hit the bottom.

Equally hilarious was the weekly Saturday matinee at the local cinema, The Regal. My attendance at this was irregular, because, in common with my mates, I was frequently banned; but I went whenever I could, and participated to the full in the entertainment on offer. This included, of course, a film – usually two films, a cartoon and the Pathe Newsreel which, alone among any organs of publicly expressed opinion, continued to labour under the impression that Britain was a great imperial power. Most of its outpourings featured the Queen and The Duke of Edinburgh in some exotic location, watching stoically as natives danced, tits wobbling up and down just out of arms' reach. The Duke must have seen more naked tits than any male who has ever lived. Maybe, he got to see the Queen's as well. The films were lurid: a cowboy or the adventures of Zorro, who was a sort of cowboy with a sword, was staple fare. However, the films, though included in the price of the ticket, were not the main point. The main point was to be in a darkened room, with no effective adult supervision, in the company of hundreds of other children, all equally intent on evil-doing.

There were attempts made to quell the ensuing riots. There was an old chap with a torch, who walked up and down the aisles making disapproving noises. There were usherettes, who wisely refrained from intervention, and restricted themselves to the sale of ice cream at the intervals. There were even moments when the management would stop the film and announce sternly,

"In the event of further disorder, this programme will cease. No refund will be made. Anyone caught will be reported to the police."

This threat was, however, never carried out, and the effect of its obvious and repeated emptiness was to goad us into further hooliganism.

An observer might have been puzzled, in a supposedly full cinema, to see a number of rows of empty seats. These seats had owners, but they were occupied in crawling beneath the rows on commando missions. Often, these were aimed at other children. A preferred feat, for those of us in balcony seats, was to steal the ice cream belonging to someone else, and hurl it over the balcony onto the stalls below. A lucky shot would land on an unsuspecting head below, often eliciting a satisfying scream.

"Wot's up?" the attendant would howl, "Wot's all that screamin'?"

We came, of course, fully armed with peashooters, and a copious supply of grey farters, with which we would attack the attendant himself.

"Who's got that bloody peashooter?" he would bawl, adding disastrously, "I cor see yer."

The price of admission was sixpence, ninepence to go upstairs. None of us ever saw much of the official entertainment, but the Saturday Matinee was the highlight of the weekend, better even than the visit to the Molyneux when the Wolves were playing at home.

It seems miraculous now that none of us came, despite our utter wildness and freedom from any effective adult supervision, to serious harm. Some of what we did – walking on iced-over pools, climbing trees and scaffolding – had obvious dangers; other activities, such as placing coins on railway lines to be run over may have entailed dangers for others. We played games of "chicken" with oncoming vehicles, and clambered on old and rusting machinery. There were, too, different kinds of harm that we evaded, though not through any instinct of self-preservation that we possessed. Our mothers warned us, of course, as have mothers through the ages, not to take sweets from strangers, and we did not, principally because no strangers ever offered them to us. From time to time, though, in the wilderness of Bacca's End, odd men would appear, and ask to see our penises. Our response was always to hurry off, and throw stones from a safe distance; Pill once, with his developing instinct for the corrupt, accepted ten shillings to pee in a man's mouth. Mickey and I were somewhat repelled by this, though we helped to spend the ten shillings. This was probably the closest we came to undesirable sexual contact: for the most part, we had no idea that such beings as paedophiles existed.

Our lives were rough, but generally carefree. We were perhaps the hardiest generation that has ever lived in England. The remains of postwar rationing ensured that we ate a balanced diet and above all that we remained "regular.". We had school milk, orange juice, cod-liver oil and California Syrup of Figs. Convenience food had not been invented, and there were no supermarkets to sell it. The day had yet to dawn when a Tesco could make billions from schemes of mass poisoning. Our mothers were convinced of the health-giving properties of milk and "best" butter, and they all cooked and administered vegetables with merciless rigour. Joints of meat were compulsory. Every Sunday lunch featured beef, lamb or pork; chicken was a luxury reserved for Christmas, and none of the meat was processed. As the week went on, cheaper items such as belly pork would appear. In general, though, we were better fed than working-class children are now. None of us were fat or puny, and illness was discouraged by our mothers. We could stand rain, heat and cold, and we were outside in all weathers, partly from preference and partly because we were not allowed in. Even now, I associate being in the house all day with illness.

I suppose I could say that my childhood, at least until the age of 12 or 13, was a happy one. My father had not then fully developed the darker traits that marred his, and our, lives later on. Unusually among working-class men at that time, he liked to spend time with his children. He had little time to spare, for he worked five full days a week and both Saturday and Sunday mornings. Then, when the weather was suitable, he would take us walking. Later, our corgi dog, Sandy, would occupy us, noisily bustling around the heels of cows, which he tried unsuccessfully to herd; or, he would play at chasing with us. He would run, snarling, dodging our attempts to catch him. Because Corgis have virtually no legs, they are extremely manoeuvrable, but also pathetically slow. It was possible to run behind Sandy and, bending, to grasp his stump of a tail. This would provoke intense paroxysms of simulated wrath, so that he would turn, with bared teeth, and then I would run, easily keeping a strategic two yards ahead of him. Once or twice, I slipped, and he was on me, barking joyously, his breath hot in my face. I would grab him with both hands to hold him back, and again the snarling would commence, for all the world as though he were intent on ripping out my throat.

My father would walk, and make my sister and me walk, for what seemed like many miles. Actually, it must never have been more than three or four, but that amounted to what he called "a good walk." He could jump a five-barred gate from a standing start, and occasionally demonstrated this feat. Once, he just failed, catching his foot on the top bar of the gate, and plunging headfirst onto the grass. It must have hurt, but he stood up immediately, scanning our faces for the slightest semblance of a grin. He found none. We were too shocked. It was as well my mother was not there. She would have laughed till she burst. The fields over which we walked then were unkempt, reclaimed industrial lands. They have since disappeared beneath roads, houses and industrial estates. They are, however, my land of lost content. I was happier on those occasional walks than I have ever been in all the years since.

Bacca's End

When we were young and ragged-arsed,
And turned our underpants around
From day to day, the world was limtless,
All that we imagined it to be.
The spoil-heaps, barely green
With sparse anaemic grass, were Alps,
The Black Hills of Dakota, the Andes
Or the Hindu Kush, the bilious trickles
Of muddy slime that passed for streams
Were torrents carrying off the soil
From Khyber or the high plateau of Tibet.
The rain-filled puddles were Alpine lakes
At the glacier's end, concealed
And sheltering undiscovered carnivores.
Armed to the teeth and desperate,
We strode the unkempt altiplano,
Hunting the Bigfoot, or in search of Eldorado,
Unobserved, beyond control, till dark
Fell like a condor on the imagined veldt
And the streetlamps puncturing the twilight
Called us home from fantasy to tea.

Schooling

Wednesfield High Street

Schooling is not a synonym for education. It is not necessarily antithetical to it, though it often appeared to be the chief professional concern of teachers to make it so. Not by any means all of what I learned as a young child came from official sources. There is a theory abroad these days that by the age of five (I think it is) an "advantaged" child hears some thirty million words more than a "disadvantaged" one. There may be more than one opinion on whether in fact this constitutes or contributes to "advantage." It depends, I should have thought, on what the words are, and how they are put together. Nevertheless, I rather doubt whether I was in this sense, though undeniably working class, "disadvantaged". Certainly, to have regular contact with my mother was not to experience linguistic deprivation, except in the sense that the language spoken was only distantly related to English.

Adults talked to me. In particular, my grandfather and, for all his contradictions and occasional cruelties, my father talked to me. I learned from my mother and grandfather about the past: the early twentieth century as they had experienced it: about the two wars, the great flu, the General Strike, the depression of the nineteen-thirties and the post-war welfare state. I learned that we had an Empire, and that this was a good thing, not only for us, but for the rest of the World too. Sometimes, in token of the benevolence of British rule, the subject peoples were allowed to call themselves a Commonwealth and to come to London in funny clothes. I learned that Winston Churchill had defeated the Germans, with help from Errol Flynn and Richard Todd, but that he was both a Tory and, in my mother's view, a "war-mongrel." I understood that this was intended to be a disparaging judgement, but I found it hard to understand why, since the most striking fact about wars was that England always won them. I knew that we had first a King and then, confusingly, a Queen and that the rather sad-looking chap sitting on a horse in the middle of Wolverhampton was a sort of foreign Royal called the Prince Consort, but I had no idea with whom he was consorting or for what purpose. I understood that we were living in a welfare state, and that this meant that one had to take cod-liver oil, and I was certainly brought up to believe that, bleak as life could sometimes seem, in winter or a wet November, things were much better than they had been. One day, my grandfather assured me, I would have letters after my name. I did not know what this meant, but I was clear that it was eminently desirable.

I knew, in other words, and so far as I remember always have known, a good deal about the world in which I lived. Unlike, apparently, many children growing up today, I had a sound if not detailed sense of twentieth century chronology. I knew who the Prime Minister was, and that Mr. Atlee and Mr. Churchill were on different sides of politics. My father and grandfather assured me that Atlee was on our side, though this always struck me as slightly doubtful. He certainly did not sound like one of us. I knew also who Jesus was, and the outline of the New Testament story.

As I grew older, I was given books that introduced me to Greek Mythology and to the tales of the Norse Gods, of whom I strongly approved, especially Thor. I think that my father occasionally read these, and other, books to us when we were very young.

My father always appeared to be interested in what, and how, we thought. He would argue some point of ethics or politics with us, and delight in demonstrating the feebleness of our arguments. I do not think he saw this as especially educative. He merely liked to argue. This was one of the reasons for his frequent altercations with my mother, who liked to row. My uncles, too, were argumentative, especially Harold, who would delight in confronting us with some doomladen pronouncement culled from the Watchtower in order to provoke a reaction. From my father I learned scepticism about the more preposterous claims of religion, and a certain skill in pointing out logical contradiction, as well as a love of argument for its own sake.

My parents were much given to sudden enthusiasms on our behalf. When I was about seven, my father without warning suddenly acquired an upright piano, and had it tuned. The tuning process fascinated me, as I had never heard a real piano played in a private house. It sounded wonderfully loud. My sister Pauline, who was not much interested, was compelled to have piano lessons. I asked to be allowed to do so as well, but was refused on the grounds that I "had no talent." Undoubtedly this was true, but I would have liked the opportunity to demonstrate ineptitude before being convicted of it.

We were sent to Sunday school and to the cubs. The latter imposition was, I believe, indirectly the fault of Roy, who wished to join the cubs, but was unwilling to go on his own. I thought it from the start entirely absurd. We sat on our haunches in a circle, replying "dob, dob, dob," to a rather bored-looking woman, known as "Arkela", who had begun this pointless exchange with the equally meaningless "dib, dib, dib." This appeared to be what passed for conversation in these circles. We learned skills useful to bush-dwellers, such as tying knots and lighting fires, though the latter we learned only in principle, since the scout-hut was a wooden structure. The tying of knots seemed to be an unnecessarily complex business. A knot, I thought, was a knot. You used one, for example, to tie a string to a bow. Not so! What I had thought was a knot turned out to be a "grannie" and people who were satisfied to tie things up with grannies were, at best, morally lax and, quite possibly, enemy sympathizers.

The cubs, it soon became clear, was an extraordinarily hierarchical organisation. Your place in the hierarchy was demoted both by where you stood in line, when your troop was lined up, and by your uniform. One boy – a tall, blond Aryan superman called, enviably, "Rod" – had three yellow stripes on his green shirt. Others had two; others again a single stripe. The majority of us had none. I was to remain stripeless for the whole of my cub career, no doubt in recognition of my inability to complete suitably morally improving knots. That career fortunately came to an end at the age of 11 when I was allowed to decide whether or not to graduate to the scouts. I had no interest in doing so. I would have preferred the sea-scouts, whose popularity at that time was unaffected by the fact that Wednesfield is about at far from the sea as it is possible to get in England, or the boys' brigade. There were, as you see, a number of these paramilitary organizations available, and they would all, for no obvious reasons, occasionally parade around the streets together. We had some vague sense that to be organized in this way came with the privilege of being an imperial power. The scouts in particular, we knew, were essential to the relief of Mafeking. However, since no one ever explained to us what kind of activity Mafeking was, or why it required relief, we were not very much the wiser.

So, I learned from these early experiences much that was partial, vague, somewhat jingoistic and certainly haphazard. From about six months after my fourth birthday, there began to be hints that some metamorphosis, of a not necessarily agreeable sort, was about to occur. My mother would say from time to time:

"Yo'll be at school soon." Then, darkly, she would add, "thank God."

Or a neighbour would ask,

"Wo 'e be at school soon?"

And mother would reply,

"Ar, thank God."

Inevitably, someone would then add, with a meaningful expression, looking at me:

"Yo'll know about it then, wo yer!"

From this, I inferred that entry to school was (a) inevitable (b) imminent and (c) unlikely to be congenial, indeed that it was an event that could be regarded as curtailing the blissful freedom of early childhood, including the freedom to freeze in unheated houses, and beginning the long, slow slide into adulthood, with the awful spectre of employment ahead, albeit distantly. I had no particular desire to grow up. It seemed to have little to offer beside the freedom to drink and smoke, neither of which appealed to me particularly at the age of four. From time to time, attempting sympathy perhaps, an adult would add, though not in a voice that suggested either conviction or the expectation of being believed:

"Yer schooldays are the best days of yer life."

Where did this idiotic cliché first arise and gain currency? It is about as true as the notion that "life begins at 40." There are some pathetic beings who see their schooldays through a romantic haze. Most, surely, see them as I do: as a kind of wry, only occasionally amusing, comedy: rather like Menander, the sort of comedy that is by no means all that funny, but is based on the proposition that we learn through suffering: "pathei mathos."

It must have been in 1952 that I began my stint of learning through suffering, just as England acquired a new queen, inaugurating a second Elizabethan era. If the history of England since then has consisted largely of anti-climax, with some high points, that could also be said of my schooling. It began inauspiciously, rose unobtrusively, and settled on a rather modest plateau.

I went first to Neachells Lane County Primary School. "Google" tells me that the school ceased to exist in 1993. Indeed, most of the schools in that part of Wednesfield have ceased to exist, through closure or amalgamation, over the last two decades, no doubt owing to a wholly understandable desire on the part of anyone living in that area not to reside there for a moment longer than absolutely necessary.

Neachells Lane was never one of the great thoroughfares; it is not easily confused with, say, the Kufurstendamm or Las Ramblas. It is, and was, a long and grubby road that sidles down past railway and canal bridges, factories and warehouses, towards Willenhall. At the Willenhall End, there was fragrantly sited what we called "the potted meat factory." It was in fact an establishment that made glue, by boiling down horses' hooves. This was not an establishment celebrated for wasting its fragrance on the desert air. When it was brewing and the wind was in the right quarter, a fetid stink of rendered flesh hung over Wednesfield, like a filthy sheet flapping on a clothesline. Neachells Lane intersected with Hart Road, where my grandparents lived, at the bottom of which was the Weldless Steel Tube Factory, adding its own fragrance of boiling tar, diesel fumes and leaking gas. By the time I went there, my parents had moved house, and I was therefore somewhat unlucky not to be sent to a slightly more favoured school, a bit nearer to our new home.

I was not of course aware that, by being allocated to Neachells Lane, I was being in any sense assigned to the ranks of the underprivileged, and my parents had no idea that the school's record of 11-plus passes was distinctly modest. My mother had herself been there, and if that should have alerted her to any deficiencies, it did not. The place itself seemed impressive enough to my five year old self, inevitably, since it was the first time I had ever been deposited in a large public building and left.

I was conscious of two things: that the architecture was vaguely, but almost certainly designedly, ecclesiastical: a high (immensely high) room with gothic arches and mullioned windows. Had I been more sophisticated, I would have expected this, since the school had been built at a time (the late Victorian Era) when schools were built with a view to assisting the Church (of England in this case) in its mission to convince humanity that this world is but a Vale of Tears. It had nothing comfortable or welcoming about it at all, only what seemed to be hundreds of children sitting at dark wooden forms, like rows of starlings on telegraph wires. There cannot of course have been literally hundreds, but neither can the reception class have held fewer than fifty children, of whom several, like me, were new. The second sensation of which I was conscious was of an overwhelming smell of cold, buttered toast. Why this should have so pervaded the chilly room, I could not say. I simply assumed that it emanated from the children themselves. Perhaps it did. Perhaps what I thought was toast was actually the smell of small bodies encased in insufficiently frequently washed underwear. If so, it was not unpleasant.

I did not, I think, immediately grasp the nature of the school day. It had not been explained to me that it would extend over several sessions, with breaks, known as "play-times," intervening. Therefore, when a bell sounded, after what seemed like weeks, and we were lined up to go out, I simply went home.

"Wot yo doin' 'ere?" said my astonished mother. "Why ay yo at school?"

"It's finished," I said.

I was marched back to the Headmistress, who I think was called Mrs Price, and sternly told off. The awesome penalties that awaited truants were explained to me, and I was asked if I wanted to set myself up as a failure in life by absconding from an institution in which I had been incarcerated For My Own Good – Mrs Price had the knack of talking in capitals. It slowly began to dawn on me that school lasted all day, every day. Now I understood the implied threat when adults had referred to my coming incarceration. From now on, this was life.

I remember very little of my infants school, other than a sense of almost permanent mystification. A great deal of time was spent learning to recite the alphabet, a feat which I could not reliably accomplish until, I think, my teens. This did not prevent my learning to read; how could it, since I believe I could already read before entering school. However, the recitation of the alphabet, combined with a sort of coarse and staccato grunting out of words that has subsequently been dignified with the appellation "phonics" were taken to be essential to literacy, presumably in an attempt to remove from the act of reading any hint of the pleasure it might otherwise have given. Not that pleasure was easily derived from the fatuous "reading schemes" that were our staple diet: biliously coloured pamphlets in which anodyne middle-class children were depicted doing uninteresting things in language which failed to excite. By the end of the infants school, I was in the second set for reading. At the end of every day of toiling half-heartedly through the annals of Janet and John, I would go home to "Nicholas Nickleby, " or "A Farewell to Arms." My experience, in other words, was precisely that of Scout, at the hands of Miss Caroline in "To Kill a Mocking-bird." To be fair, though, if one must be fair, it is hard to see how, with such enormous classes, individual needs could have been catered for. I was a bright boy, keen to learn, but not bright in the ways that led to success in primary education as then organized. I was wayward, eccentric, intent on pursuing those things I was interested in, not those my teachers wished me to be interested in.

I had only one intellectual accomplishment to my credit, and that involved deception. On one occasion, my teacher asked,

"Who knows how to tell the time?"

Of course, we all put our hands up, not wishing to court the public denunciation that often followed a confession of ignorance. It seemed to me odd then, and it seems odd still, that teachers so often expected you to know things that it might have been thought their province to teach you, then upbraided you for not possessing the knowledge they had not attempted to impart. It similarly struck me as odd that, at regular intervals throughout my schooling, teachers would write on my report,

"He shows no interest in what he does."

All too often, this was true, but I was unable to understand why it should be to my discredit, when the failure was surely theirs.

There was of course a risk inherent in claiming knowledge you did not actually possess.

"David Singleton," said my teacher, "Go down to the school hall and see what time it is by the school clock."

Evidently, the morning had begun to weigh as heavily on her as on her charges. I was thus in some difficulty, but off I went to scan the dial of the clock in the school hall – and I worked out how to read it! I claim this as an accomplishment of the first order. I not only secured the correct information, but evaded the penalty that would surely have followed being caught in deception. The momentousness of this feat went of course totally unrecognized:

"Thank you, David. Now go and sit down."

And so, I went to rejoin the other mute inglorious Miltons in reading group two, all still beavering away at Volume 27 of the adventures of the egregious Janet and John – or Jack and Jill. They were wholly interchangeable.

Of course, we did more than learn how to read. We also did arithmetic and lots of it. We had books with pages divided into minute squares into which we attempted to fit numbers. Mine always overlapped, and lurched drunkenly down the page. My efforts were regularly anathematized:

"Scruffy! Poor presentation! Try to be neater!"

It was quickly discovered that I " took no pride in my work." This accusation has always seemed to me to be on a par with the condemnatory comment that appeared rather frequently on my later school reports: "he shows no interest in the work." Though often true, I could not and cannot see why that should count to my discredit. Surely there was some onus on the teacher to instil interest or, in this case, "pride." In fact, I was not being deliberately careless. I am simply clumsy and ham-fisted, quite unable to be tidy in any aspect of my life. I was not therefore demonstrating a lack of "pride," so much as a lack of ordinary competence. My fine motor skills were as well-honed as a steam-roller.

I have said that I remember very little of my infants school. I think I was probably very bored there, but I do not recollect resenting that. After all, I had been warned that the central purpose of school was to prepare me for the Vale of Tears that constituted adult life. I am if anything grateful that I learned early on to expect little of institutional provision, least of all excitement; that was to be got from the life of the imagination, from play and above all from reading. I do remember rather vividly the end of this particular rite of passage: I recall Mickey running home yelling,

"We're seniors! We're seniors!"

And smacking any passing heads that came within reach, and were low enough to be smacked safely. I was not so euphoric.

Moving to the junior school meant that a stage in my life had come to an end, and I had reached the age, which seemed to me a considerable one, of seven. After all, I reflected, human beings lived approximately one hundred years (I had been told this by an optimist). It followed that I had only ninety-three left. I would consider this morosely at night in my bedroom, as I studied a crack in the plaster that imagination and approaching sleep could convert into a Protean variety of shapes.

I do not know why I became thus obsessed with mortality. My sense of time was much the same as that of any child: when I left the infants for the last time, what I was most conscious of was the sheer glorious, languorous length of the holiday before me. Six weeks? It might as well have been six decades, or six centuries. For the moment, and for the foreseeable future, there was only the endless, school-less summer.

There is, I believe, a form of depression that is triggered in Autumn. I think I have heard it referred to as SAD. I should imagine that it is, in varying degrees, universal. Received opinion has it that it is connected with the fading of the light, with the associated production of vitamins. In fact, it stems from a racial memory of the return to school each September. The first harbinger would be the start of the football season; then there would be the final test match; mothers would announce cheerfully to each other,

"They'll soon be back at school, then."

"Ar, bloody good job, too."

Then school clothes would be tried on, and discovered, amid much cursing, to have been outgrown. Others, two sizes too large, would be purchased or, worse, made in order to be "grown into." Of course, one never did. I was known to be "hard on clothes"; nothing survived long enough to be grown into.

And soon, instead of weeks, you were counting off the days, with a sense of deepening despair, like Doctor Faustus, with

106

Mephistopheles standing by, alarm clock in hand. Then, we were juniors and to prove it we went into Miss Bolus' class – she who lived not far from us, though in circumstances of much greater respectability. Her house was said, respectfully, to be private. She seemed to us to be older than a human being could possibly be, grey-haired, sober and stern. We were, I think, her final class. At the end of the year, she retired after forty years at Neachells Lane. The Head, Mr.Baxter, made a speech about her, in which he said:

"Forty years! You can do a lot in 40 years, and Miss Bolus has done it."

We waited for him to enlighten us further, but he failed to supply further information. Given that these events occurred 57 years ago, I must assume that Miss Bolus is no longer with us. I have occasionally wondered what she thought of her final class, and whether she ever heard what became of any of us.

So far as I am aware, all of us have led lives of effortless lack of distinction. My sister recently showed me a photograph of my class. I could name only five or six. Winston Pollock was of course immediately recognizable, for the colour of his skin, rather than the imagined dimensions of his testicles. There was Arnold Hope, who looked exactly as such a name would lead you to expect: stoop-shouldered, small, anxious and studious. He was probably, with me, though more obviously so, the most bookish member of the class. My own mates: Royston, Mickey and Ian were there, remarkable only for their identically evasive expressions. So too was Tony Humphries, who was already improbably handsome – a fact which he exploited fully in later years. Of the girls, the only one I could identify with certainty was Cynthia Wellings, who died at 16, never recovering from the anaesthetic administered for a minor operation. I do not know what the occasion of the photograph was, but we were all wearing white shirts or blouses, which looked clean. Unusually also, all of us had clearly been made to do something with their hair. Mostly, this was simply to plaster it down. Royston, however, had achieved a small sculptural triumph. He looked as though he was balancing a loaf on his head. I look as though I had just been instructed to stand up straight with my shoulders back – people were always saying that sort of thing to me. The result was that I am looking straight up into the air, so that only my neck and chin can be seen. They were still, in those days, easily distinguishable from each other.

I remember Miss Bolus as "strict". This was, so far as we were concerned, the mark of a good teacher, to be feared and respected. For challenge, excitement and fascination we did not look. I think it is true of most children that they learn very early to have low expectations of adults. Certainly it was true of us. We expected to be bored, but we felt that we ought to be kept in order. Miss Bolus, of course, taught us the entire curriculum, except for music: the BBC did that. We listened each week to a music programme for schools, which did much to ensure that the pleasures of music were largely denied to me till my late teens. I do not recall doing very much science, or much art. History was dates, and the Kings and Queens of England, and geography was places and, for some reason, Masai warriors. On at least four occasions in my school career, I was shown a film of Masai warriors dancing and waving spears, when not herding what appeared to be half-starved cattle. Presumably, this was in Kenya, which was one of those gratifyingly large areas on the globe still in those days coloured red. I have no idea what was the origin of the obsession of the English education system with the Masai, but certainly we knew more about life in distant outposts of the Empire than we did of daily life in, say, France.

Miss Bolus, as teachers then did, read to us. This was immensely preferable to our reading aloud, which most of us did so execrably that it was impossible even to follow the outlines of a plot, let alone catch any nuance. I remember, we had "Treasure Island," which I promptly asked for, and got, as a Christmas present. She also read to us a story, about smuggled dynamite, written by a former pupil, who had gone on to Birmingham University. That will seem a commonplace enough accomplishment to people of the current generation, but for my school it was an unprecedented achievement. Miss Bolus explained to us:

"Maureen went to university. University is where you go when you are brilliant."

She invested the word "brilliant" with such feeling that we were left in no doubt of the exceptional nature of what Maureen had done. She came in to help, late in the year, and I remember her as a quietly encouraging girl, wearing her "brilliance" in all modesty. The story was, I thought, at least as good as the published stuff we read, and I suspect that Maureen may have been the only one of Miss Bolus' pupils ever to get to university. The thought of being officially recognized as "brilliant" greatly appealed to the element of intellectual snobbery already present in my character, and from that point on, going to university began to coalesce as a vague aspiration in my thoughts. It was not of course a sufficiently firm intention actually to engender any change in behaviour, such as working harder, misbehaving less, or reading what was prescribed, rather than what I fancied, or what my Dad happened to have just read.

Other than Miss Bolus, the teacher I remember best was Mr.Roberts, who stood out as being both male and Welsh. A great many of my teachers over the years were Welsh, to the extent that I imagined that only two professions, those of coalminer and teacher, were open to that oppressed and much-disliked nation. Mr.Roberts was not "strict." He aspired to be, but he lacked the knack. Where Miss Bolus could maintain order with the movement of an eyebrow, he was unable to do so with a loud voice and a strong right hand. His weapon of choice was the ruler. We would queue, giggling idiotically at the front of the class, for raps over the knuckles for such crimes as drawing a moustache on a photograph of Queen Victoria, or throwing pencils, or "not trying." What I most vividly remember of these lessons was completing page after page of identical maths problems and either getting them all right, or making the same mistake 50 times over. I don't think I much objected to this, or to reciting our tables, because it was easy, repetitive and involved no thought. Children do not much mind being bored. They expect it. They hate being made to think far more. Fortunately, this was not an ordeal to which I was at all frequently subjected. I had a good memory, and this was all you needed to do well in practically every subject. With neither effort, nor thought, I was top of my class, my only rivals being the redoubtable Arnold Hope and a fat girl with the unfortunate name of Gillian Wopples.

When I describe Arnold as "a rival," I do not mean to suggest that I felt any antipathy towards him. I did not. He lived up the road from my grandparents, and I saw him quite often, and occasionally went to his house. He was a gentle soul, who kept rabbits and guinea-pigs, and read a lot. I would have liked to make more of a friend of him than I did, but he had the appearance of someone who was not robust. He was thin, pale and, if not already incipiently balding, he lacked the coarse mop of hair most of us possessed. He did not go out very much, and certainly never played football or cricket, which occupied much of my time, but was instead, interesting and thoughtful. By some travesty, of the sort then common, he failed the eleven-plus. I have often thought about this. I should have liked to have had him as a friend at grammar school, but more than that, I suspect that this obvious injustice was a personal tragedy. I do not know what happened to him. After leaving primary school, I saw him only once, when he came to the grammar school as one of a bunch of aspiring 13 plus entries, I imagine for interview. By then, I was too shy to speak to him, and he was too overwhelmed by the occasion to speak to me, but his presence excited me with the prospect of gaining an ally. However, he never appeared after that.

For me, Arnold encapsulates in his person the case against grammar schools. His initial failure at eleven was in itself a travesty. He was a bright and bookish boy, who enjoyed learning; he was more studious than I was, and just as bright. There was provision for the system to rectify the injustice, but if failed to do so. He

110

therefore languished, at the same school my mother had attended and which retained the qualities that had made her education the failure it was. The assessment at eleven was a lottery, and once selected, your course was mapped out for you as surely as if the distinction had been between black and white in the southern United States.

Of course, we didn't know that then, in that September of 1954, when we entered the junior school at Neachells Lane. We were, after all, only seven, and at that point none of us had heard of the eleven –plus (though my mother had cryptically referred to a "scholarship exam," as a distant and formidable ordeal), much less knew of its significance. We now had entry to the juniors playground, which was a vast concrete plain, curving towards the centre, with a drain that occasionally became blocked, to create a large and impromptu reservoir. On either side of the playground there were two covered areas for rainy days, one for boys and one for girls, with the respective toilets attached. The division between boys and girls was absolute and unthinking. I scarcely remember speaking to a girl at junior school and, had I done so, there would have been no reply other than a look of contempt. We sat on either side of the classroom, and boys dominated most of the playground, playing football or cricket, with girls to one side, engrossed in their complex skipping games. In the playground itself, somewhat off-centre, there was a brick coal-shed. Our football games eddied around this construction: indeed, it was an added skill in playground football to employ the shed as an additional player, rounding the opposition by playing a one-two off the wall; the wall was perhaps the only member of the team from whom a return pass could confidently be expected. On the whole, once you had the ball, you retained it as long as you could. The need to round the shed added, of course, greatly to the chances of collision, and it was there, when I was nine, that I broke my nose for the first time, racing full-tilt into a smaller boy moving equally fast, with head lowered. The shower of blood I emitted gave me, I recall, heroic status for a little while, particularly because I remember I did not "blart." I was too shocked, and in any event the pain came later. Our immediate concern was not to seek medical attention, but to disguise from any responsible adults the fact that an accident had occurred. Our experience was that all incidents, however painful and fortuitous, were regarded by the powers that be as opportunities for the allocation of blame. So, two of my mates went with me to the cloakroom and, as best they could, mopped the blood from my face. This had a surprisingly dramatic event on the cloakroom; it looked like a recently abandoned battlefield. I went off to class as usual, attempting to be as stoical as possible in the face of the rapidly increasing pain. It was, of course, useless: characteristically, the girls at once informed on me:

"Please Miss, have you seen David Singleton's face?"

"Come here David. Good heavens! What have you been doing?"

"Please Miss, it wor me."

"Don't be stupid. That is your face, isn't it? And that is your nose twice its usual size. Michael, what happened to David?"

"Please Miss, a boy ran into 'is nose. It was an accident. We was playin' football round the shed."

In the event, the feared reprisals did not take place. I was instead taken to the outpatients' department of the Royal Hospital, Wolverhampton in no less a vehicle than the headmaster's car, he having first checked carefully that the flow of blood had ceased. Thither my mother was summoned, and arrived, complaining of the inconvenience and worry.

"Ah dow know, our David, yow dow 'arf worry me!"

This was characteristic. All injuries and illnesses were not afflictions from which her children might be thought to suffer, so much as malevolent or careless attempts to cause her worry or inconvenience.

I was duly x-rayed, and felt a swell of pride and consciousness of a new glamour, when the verdict of a broken nose was proclaimed. Nothing was done about it, other than to prescribe aspirin for the pain "if there was any." I heard this with some indignation. Of course, there was pain. You try having some bullet-headed moron run full tilt into your proboscis and you see if there is any pain, Mate. And also with some disappointment. I appreciated the difficulty of putting the nose in a sling, but I had entertained some hope that my entire face might be bandaged, leaving only my eyes visible, like the invisible man. Sadly, it was not to be, and my attempts next day to persuade my mother that I was in too much pain to go to school fell on stony ground.

As I have said, the other building in the playground was the toilet block, about as distant from the classrooms as the available space permitted. In winter, the walk to and from the boys' lavatory constituted an Arctic ordeal of Oatesian rigour. No one who has not lowered his trousers outside in January and placed his quivering cheeks on frozen wood can conceive of the sheer sensual pleasure of knowing that he will never have to do so again. In summer. the lavatory presented a different kind of challenge, olfactory, rather than climatic. The small of stale urine, and worse, competed with the miasma drifting off the potted meat factory to cast its peculiar fragrance over that part of South Staffordshire.

It was, after all, 1954. There was a new Queen on the throne. Mr.Churchill, though sadly reduced from the hero of the war years, was still Prime Minister; Len Hutton was captaining England at cricket, and there was only one television channel, which gave you what was good for you, mostly films of a pot being shaped upon a wheel, it seemed. It was long before the invention of health and safety – and yet we were all indecently healthy, and if no one cared very much about our safety, that at least gave us room to grow up.

It was 1954, and September. The classroom was full of autumn display, much of it incomprehensible to us children of the industrial Midlands: pine-cones, oak-leaves, ripened wheat; for we were preparing for Harvest Festival, for all the world as though we had been Croatian peasants, for whom such a concept might have had some reality. Do schools still celebrate harvest festival? If they do, the music alone makes it a pity, for surely the hymns are among the most sentimental, cloying and trivial in the whole of Hymns Ancient and Modern. "We plough the fields and scatter," is possibly the worst, though we improved it somewhat by the substitution of the word "scarper" for "scatter," and as we grew older "scattering the good seed on the land" came to acquire a new and more urgent meaning. "All things bright and beautiful" was almost equally nauseating in its combination of relentless cheerfulness with dubious theology. Were we to believe that God was responsible only for the bright and beautiful, while someone else got the blame for the dark, the malevolent and the ugly? I did not, of course, voice these concerns. All that was expected was compliance: not necessarily belief, and certainly not discussion. The fact was that the 1944 Education Act, representing as it did a compromise between the state and the churches, had enshrined religious education and worship as part of the education of every English child. My school took this bigoted nonsense seriously, as most did, I imagine. We therefore spent the fleeting hours of our early youth intoning words we did not comprehend, to tunes we could not stand, in praise of a deity in whose existence we were given no reason to believe.

Much later, when I was at grammar school, I plucked up the courage to say to our RE teacher, who was in this case the headmaster,

"Sir, why do people actually believe in God?"

He looked at me with astonishment, oddly, since it cannot have been the first time he had heard the question.

"Don't you think, Singleton," he replied, "that our lives would be somewhat meaningless in the absence of a divine providence?"

I made no reply, but it did seem to me at the time, and does now, that the question leads to a rather different conclusion than the one the speaker was evidently expecting.

Music, of a sort, played a considerable role in the education we received at Neachells Lane. We had hymn practice once a week, and for a year we also had singing lessons. I enjoyed these, as I have always enjoyed singing, though it was often the exercise I appreciated, rather than the music. The teacher had a preference for the English baroque, and we therefore spent rather more time than was necessary, trilling:

"Nymphs and shepherds, come away, come away, come, come, come, co-o-ome away."

Which is a pleasant enough way to waste a few minutes that might otherwise have been spent solving thirty-seven more undemanding problems in arithmetic, but is otherwise not much use to a growing boy. Or, even worse, we asked the question:

"Did you not see my lady, go down the garden singing,

Silencing all the songbirds, and setting the alleys ringing?"

Alleys? The word conjured, for us town children, a picture somewhat remote from the Watteauesque idyll that Handel presumably had in mind, and which he conjures up in his music.

There, in a nutshell, was a feature of education that added to its colour, even as it limited its effectiveness. Our teachers were outrageously prone to believe that we understood far more than we actually did, or that our understanding was in fact aligned to whatever it was they were trying to communicate. As often as not, this was far from the case. So, for example, when we said the Lord's Prayer, as we did every day, what I heard was:

Our Father. Witch-art in heaven.

Allowed be thy name.

This made, I agree, no sense, but neither, so far as I was concerned, did the original. When we got to "Forgive us our trespasses," I thought only of our scrumping expeditions, which indeed counted as "trespasses," but may not have been entirely what was meant. In geography, I heard "meander" as "me and 'er" and for some time imagined that the line of the equator was more than merely imaginary. And yet, I do not recollect a teacher ever asking us if we understood, or otherwise checking our understanding. Our teachers were kinder than my mother's. They greeted incomprehension with a pitying smile, rather than a rap on the knuckles, and there was no bench for the "dunces" to sit on, in deserved and perpetual humiliation. But we were in no doubt that, when we failed to understand, it was essentially our fault, occasioned by our stupidity or lack of interest in what we were doing .

It must have been an unrewarding job, to be a primary school teacher in those days, though it was without the pressure of accountability it has since accrued. I think of Mr.Roberts. He was a fit, good-looking man who seemed to us to be of immense antiquity. I suppose he cannot actually have been more than 40. He taught us how to play cricket, though he had about as much knowledge of the game as you would expect of a Welshman; other than that, he took us through our daily sums, handwriting practice, spelling lessons and compositions with more determination than appearance of enjoyment. He had done the same each year for perhaps 20 years, and could look forward to 20 years more of the same before, like Miss Bolus, retiring to the sound of a Laodicean eulogy from some future Headmaster. Apart from Mr.Baxter, he was the only man on the staff, and had failed to locate the bottom of the promotion ladder, and each day he could expect to be confronted with 40 or so indifferent and uncomprehending faces. It must, though of course I did not think so at the time, have been a deeply unsatisfying way to make a less than lucrative living. And yet, he remained a genial man, who rapped our knuckles with his ruler more as a game than in a serious attempt to inflict pain. I think he enjoyed the fact that we were inventively naughty. For him, as for us, it helped to stave off boredom.

Our female teachers were equally benevolent. They smiled; they spoke kindly to us; when they chastised us, it was with evident regret. Those of them who were married were inevitably married to other teachers. They lived in "private" houses, mostly not in Wednesfield. A few partook of the suburban glories of Tettenhall, or Compton: places that were to us merely names, surrounded by the glamour of unimaginable wealth. I pictured Tettenhall as consisting of roads in which house after house exactly replicated that of Mr.Griffiths the coal merchant. This was the grandest house I knew, with a curving drive, sweeping lawns and – wonder of wonders – a stream trickling through the grounds. To own a stream! This was wealth beyond conception. I remember walking past there one day with Mickey.

"Look," he said, "They'm 'aving tea on the lawn. That's something we'll never 'ave."

This was how I imagined my teachers lived, as creatures from another world.

Unfortunately, for all their kindness, I think that this was also their view. There was something condescending in their kindness, something pitying in the lack of optimism with which they viewed our capacity, not, admittedly, extreme, to learn. We were our parents' children, and our parents had failed to make good their escape from what we then called "the working class." We were not especially poverty-stricken, as poverty was then judged, in the days before designer labels and expensive gizmos. Stretching a point only slightly, we could have been said to belong to what are now

called, with a different style of patronage, "hard-working families."
In an expansive mood, a commentator might even have said that
we were the "salt of the earth," but it was not to be expected that
we would rise much beyond the stratum in which the good Lord,
in his infinite wisdom, had caused us to be born. We would go
from Neachells Lane to the local secondary modern schools and
graduate from there, if we were lucky, to an apprenticeship or, if
we were not, to unskilled or semi-skilled work in office or factory.
Only the "brilliant" went to University, and if brilliance could not
be wholly excluded from the realms of possibility, it was certain
that it was not detected in Neachells Lane very often.

We were, in other words, like millions of other children: we had
poor expectations of ourselves and were entirely unconscious of the
equally poor aspirations others entertained on our behalf. We, our
parents and our teachers were largely unconscious of the great
social changes, post-war, that were beginning to change British
society. When, with varying degrees of reverence, we had watched
the Coronation in 1953, we had no premonition of the extent to
which deference would become outmoded, and respect, not only for
the royal family, but for all manifestations of authority, would be
eroded. We had an aristocrat for a Prime Minister, and could not
have foreseen that the next, and last, time we would see a nobleman
so employed he would be required to renounce his title and be
treated as a figure of ridicule. We had no inkling of the long-term
decline of British manufacturing industry. Those of us who expected
to spend a working life at the Weldless Steel Tube, could not foresee
a day when the great factory would cease to exist. All of our parents
had voted for Mr.Atlee after the war, and we already took for
granted those aspects of the welfare state that were established
between 1945 and 1951, but 1951 had brought what seemed to be
a restoration of the old order, and some of the old faces, and there
was nothing about Eden, MacMillan and Butler to suggest social
revolution. Margaret Thatcher was, of course, unheard of.

We were, had we known it, living through the beginnings of a
great change, but we did not know it, and our teachers did not

118

know it. Their aspiration for us was that we continue, decently, much as we were, and as our parents had been: educated enough to cope with semi-skilled work and to meet the bureaucratic demands of the state: to complete income tax forms and applications for benefit. For boys, there was of course still the looming prospect of National Service, guaranteed to interrupt any post-16 education or training we might have. As I moved, later, into my teens, this became a real, if occasional, worry.

Decency mattered. Much of our primary school education centred upon the teaching, by exhortation, example and, where necessary, enforcement, of decent moral values. In school assemblies, we were regularly urged to think of "those less fortunate than ourselves," even though we experienced some difficulty in conceiving who they might be. The notion of service figured prominently: we were encouraged to participate in charities. Later, there was a degree of persuasion to look for careers in the public service. Christianity was reinterpreted for us as a form of primitive social work: Jesus himself was a jolly good chap, whose life was full of instances of helping people "less fortunate than himself." It was not expected that we would actually raise people from the dead, and such exotic items as lepers, prostitutes and men possessed by devils were hard to find in Wednesfield, but we were exhorted nevertheless to find daily acts of kindness, whether solicited or not, to perform. For me, this was not a problem; my mother could be relied upon to demand such assistance on rather more than a daily basis.

Preposterously, we were taught to think of the history of Britain as a manifestation of decency writ large. David Livingstone, for example, figured a great deal more prominently than Job Charnock; Florence Nightingale was far more familiar than Cecil Rhodes. Mary Seacole was unheard of in those days, for disreputable reasons. Britain, we were asked to believe, had acquired an Empire out of humanity, a desire to help others "less fortunate than ourselves" and a capacity for heroic self-sacrifice. Thus, the successful struggle against Nazi Germany had been a service to humanity (as indeed it was), not just a fight for national survival, and we were not encouraged to notice that the effect of that struggle had been to leave half of Europe and a great deal of the rest of the world under a different, and hardly more tolerable, yoke of oppression. Too often, it appeared, the world had responded to our selfless assistance with rank ingratitude. The Boer War was an example, both of this, and of the tendency of our enemies to take an unsporting advantage, by demonstrating superior tactics or greater military competence. The Indian Mutiny , with its slaughter of women and children, just showed you what happened when the British were overcome and the natives ran amok.

We were taught that the greatest of virtues was heroic sacrifice, even where it was associated with rank incompetence. General Gordon figured in the national Pantheon alongside General Wolfe, Sir Thomas Moore and Horatio Nelson. The ruthlessly successful, such as Marlborough and Wellington, by comparison, earned only a chilly respect. There was something slightly un-English about supreme professional competence. So, we heard far less of Shackleton than of Scott. Hillary and Tenzing were of course heroes, because of the patriotic elan demonstrated by a successful ascent of Everest in Coronation Year, only slightly mitigated by the reflection that neither of them was actually English. Still, even at that moment of ultimate success, we spared a thought for Mallory and Irvine: brave, idiotic men staggering towards certain death in tweed jackets. What could be more English? It made your heart swell with pride. We did not know it, but we were a mere half dozen years away from "Beyond the Fringe," when these attitudes would dissolve in the acid of youthful satire:

"The time has come, Perkins, for a futile sacrifice."

Whatever we were being educated for, it was not success in an increasingly difficult and competitive world. Service to others was the ideal. We were taught to be modest, self-effacing, uncompetitive. If we achieved, and we were expected to achieve, very little in life, it was enough if we behaved decently.

In this sense, our teachers were good people. They believed in the virtues they tried to inculcate in us, and for the most part believed that they exemplified them in their own lives. They were not hypocrites. They would all have been shocked to be told that I believed, as I now do, that they were in fact leading quite a cushy, middle-class life, not much given to reflection and uninterrupted by serious work, in which they taught the same lessons each year to largely apathetic, but compliant, pupils, without, for more than one or two, communicating the pleasure that there is in learning. They were all decent, humdrum people made soft and lazy through the lack of accountability that arises from contact day to day with children who have neither driving ambitions, nor powerful advocates.

Ah, but "your schooldays are the best days of your life." It would, if I am to go by my own experience, be a seriously impoverished life of which this was true. The principal emotion I recall was that of boredom; I remember nothing from any lesson that challenged or excited me. Little was allowed to impinge upon our dreary routine from the world outside. For God's sake, in 1953, Francis Crick and Jim Watson had unlocked the secret of life! You would have thought some mention of this would have obtruded upon the pallid nature study that passed, in our school, for science. However, the life-cycle of the frog was what was on the syllabus, so we collected frogspawn and observed tadpoles in a tank, without ever having the slightest inkling that there were billions of double helixes inside the animals that controlled this and every other living process. I think I would have been interested to know that, but I heard nothing of it until 1962, when Crick and Watson were awarded the Nobel Prize.

The Suez crisis also happened when I was at primary school, and I was dimly aware of it from the TV news. This now seems to me as significant an event in British history as, say, the fall of Quebec – or, more relevantly, of Singapore. It was the last serious attempt by Britain to assert itself as an Imperial power. No, I haven't forgotten the Falklands; heroically fought, irresponsibly embarked upon, outrageously lucky and atypical only in being, for a time, successful; but surely that was no more than the dead spasms of a decapitated chicken. And Suez was more than that. The Prime Minister who got us into the mess was none other than Anthony Eden, the beau ideal of diplomats, the crown prince, the matinee idol who had chosen parliament instead of Hollywood: Eton and the House, the Military Cross: soldier and gentleman. His behaviour during the crisis showed the morality of a cheap shyster. He lied to anyone from whom it mattered to conceal the truth: to the House of Commons, his colleagues, our allies and the world. Did he even lie to the Queen? They will never tell us. It was the single most powerful demonstration that if the traditional British ruling class was not yet finished, it ought to be. It was as treacherous as anyone else, just not very good at getting away with it.

Again, none of this impinged upon our education. We continued to live in a world of repetitive exercises in maths and English and of comforting stories about what a fine thing it was to be British (but also, what a responsibility, for as we were often reminded, "where there is privilege, there is also responsibility.") We nodded sagely at that, we children living in a world that was changing in ways our school was determined to prevent us from knowing: a world more dangerous than ever before (like many others, when I came to know of such matters, I expected to die in a nuclear holocaust), but also full of exciting possibilities and great discoveries. We continued, however, to live in an England in which Alfred burnt the cakes, and England expected every man to do his duty.

Fortunately, there were occasional interruptions and diversions. There were, for example, trips, some of which had a vaguely educational function, other than to give the teachers a less than well-earned rest. Once, we were taken to Dudley Zoo. It was not my first visit, but it was the first time I remember having seen bears. I do not understand the sentimental popularity that surrounds bears. They – and particularly the polar bears – seemed to me quite awe-inspiring creatures, far from the images of Rupert or Paddington Bear; not that either of those had detained me unduly. Most of my reading had been adult for as long as I could remember.

On another occasion, we were transported by coach – which we called a "charabanc" – To Weston super Mare. I do not remember this as a great success. It is a long way by coach from Wolverhampton to the West Country, and coaches were not then the luxurious vehicles they have subsequently become. They swayed – only a little, but enough to disturb the equilibrium – and they appeared to have a device for pumping diesel fumes into the passenger space. I was not myself sick, but many of my class-mates were, so that we marked our journey to the South-West by little lakes of puke left beside the roadside; when, that is, the sufferer succeeded in alighting from the coach before the demands of human frailty became too insistent. Weston super Mare had been billed to us as a seaside resort – and indeed the very name gives credence to that view. In our naivety, we believed that one of the characteristic features of the seaside might perhaps have been the presence of water, preferably briny and in considerable quantities. Not so in Weston. There is a poem by Kipling which begins beautifully:

What is a woman that you thus forsake her,

And the hearth and the home acre

To set out on the old grey widow-maker?

I know nothing about the circumstances of the composition of this poem, but I can vouch for the certainty that it was not written at Weston at low tide. Of the "old grey widow-maker" there was no sign, other than perhaps a faint glimmering on the horizon that some, sharper-eyed than I, claimed to be able to discern. What there was, was mud: black, glistening, stinking mud, with seagulls over it and occasionally landing on it. It appeared to us that the very existence of the Atlantic Ocean might itself be a myth, and that it might after all be possible to walk to America.

"Oi, Miss, there ay no sea," lamented Royston.

"Yes, there is, Royston Evans. It's just that the tide's out."

"Well, when's it coming back."

"Not till about eight o clock this evening." It was then about one.

"So we wow see it then?"

"Not this time, I am afraid."

"Not this time!" None of us had ever been there before, and the chances of any of us returning were, one felt, receding by the minute. This only went to confirm the irrationality of all things adult: to inflict upon us a puke-ridden journey, in order to visit a seaside resort with no bloody sea. Most of us were not at that epoch familiar with the poetic phrase "as sick as a parrot," but it perhaps described our state of mind with more than usual accuracy.

Of course, a black and evil-smelling plain of mud represented, for a few of us, an irresistible challenge, just as the frozen wastes of the Antarctic do to a few spirits in each generation, eager for adventure, or simply tired of life. The emphatic prohibition by Mr.Roberts on venturing onto what he optimistically called "the sands" merely rendered that challenge wholly irresistible. I did not participate, for no better reason than that I was hungry, and could smell fish and chips, but four boys, Royston among them, ventured forth, and were soon specks in the distance in search, like Xenophon's ten thousand, of the sea. It must have been with a sinking heart that our teachers saw their distant figures, when they returned from what must have felt like a well-earned lunch; when the quartet failed to reappear by five-o-clock when the coach was due to depart, it must have felt as though a career-threatening disaster had occurred.

Actually, it hadn't. They had grown bored fairly quickly at the prospect of mile after mile of mud and sand. They had merely returned to shore a mile or so away, out of sight, and had not listened to the time of departure. They were an hour late; it might have been more, but when they returned, it was not to a hero's welcome. Their stock with staff was predictably low; but their peers too blamed them for the prolongation of a day that had proved almost as tedious as a day at school.

Four years is not a large proportion of the life of an adult. To an eleven year old, it is an age. Neachells Lane took up much of my waking life. I studied there, when study was unavoidable, played there, bought sherbert and penny lollipops at the shop over the road, and had all my friends there. I had my teeth inspected there, and was condemned to the dentist. I was prescribed my first set of spectacles there: round ones with brown frames. I thought they made me look intelligent, but was unable to persuade anyone else that this was so. I fought, and beat, the first boy who called me "specky four-eyes." My reading age was assessed there, and found to be so high as almost to place me in the geriatric category. I walked there every day, and ran home every day, often pausing at the field on Alfred Squire Road, where we had made a tunnel, and where, it was alleged rats, and even foxes, could sometimes be seen. I did not think of my stay at Neachells Lane as a stage in my life, because I was at the age when everything has the illusion of permanence. I would always be there; my mother would always be there to go home to; my grandparents would always be in Hart Road. It was how things had always been, and I was generally content with how they were. I was, it was true, often bored, but I was also lazy enough to accept boredom as the price of not being forced to try too hard.

But it wasn't permanent. As a child, you feel your world is stable, but in your heart of hearts you know the adult world, in its hunger for recruits, is always working to move things – and you – on. The world turns, and you turn with it. At the age of ten we all became aware of the imminence of change. Some welcomed the prospect;

125

some feared it; most did both. Our lessons began to change. Instead of problems and exercises written on the board, we began to be given official-looking papers, covered with sums, puzzles, word-exercises and the like, and we were urged to do these with a new intensity. Somehow, it appeared that our future depended on our ability to excel at these vaguely interesting games. We were, we realized, practising like athletes for some trial, by engaging in intellectual endeavours that had no relationship whatever, so it appeared, to the education we had received up to that point. I was good at all this: among the best, but no better than several others, especially the girls. Eventually, there came a day when we all trooped off – absit omen! – to Wood End Secondary Modern School, to do more of the same exercises. I knew that my cousin Roy was doing the same thing at Ward's Bridge, on the other side of the Essington Canal, and with magnificent disdain for logic, inferred that all other ten year olds in the country were doing the same thing, on the same day. This was it! The great day! The day of spine-tingling tension, sweaty palms and squeaky bums. Except that it wasn't. None of us cared much about it. We didn't expect to pass, and we had no clear idea of what passing might mean. It was just another aberration dreamt up by adults to occupy our time.

Moving on.

The way we were

A long time ago, a friend of mine, not long married but still at that point childless, and therefore flush with the temporary wealth that comes from two incomes, decided to treat his parents to a foreign holiday. His wife advised somewhere beery and cheerful, where bacon sandwiches were easily available and English was widely spoken: Lido di Jesolo, perhaps, or the Costa del Sol. But he was an artist, an art historian and a teacher, and he was intent on widening horizons and opening up unexplored possibilities. One of the curses of upward social mobility is that it sometimes snares the young in the delusion that they can educate their parents. So it was with him. He chose to go to Florence. It is, of course, the most marvellous of cities, though you will search there in vain for a bacon sandwich, but for someone who has rarely been much further from Holmfirth (my friend is, I am obliged to confess, a Yorkshireman) than Huddersfield, it is likely to be something of a shock. The cultural distance between "Compo's Caff" and the Enoteca Pinchiorri is about as large a one as it is possible to imagine, while still remaining in Europe.

In the event, the holiday went off alright. It was not a life-changing experience for the elderly couple, but with much forbearance on all sides the relationships survived without major damage. There were moments of embarrassment, as when a crowd of tourists gathered around my friend in the Accademia, as he was explaining why the hands of the David were deliberately out of proportion. His mother interrupted, her voice effortlessly projected to reach all corners of the room:

"Well, I think his bloody legs are out of proportion, too." Then she thought a moment.

"Course, I've only got yer Dad to go by."

There were, however, few such moments. The four of them flew home and collected the car at Manchester Airport. On the way home, my friend heard his father say....

"Ee, Mother, we've been to some very interesting places, but there's none of them so nice as this."

Her agreement was equally enthusiastic.

My friend was deflated, but he should not have been. The attachment to home and its immediate surroundings is one of the strongest emotions we possess. Even now, the great majority of people in the UK spend their lives within five miles of the place where they were born, and feel something beyond loyalty and closer to unconditional love for it. I was once told by a headteacher in Stoke that teachers never left the area because Stoke "is such a nice place to live." It was not immediately obvious to the objective observer that this was so, but it appears to be what most people feel about their home. My wife and I live about five miles from where she lived as a child, for example, in Bolton, a town that has nothing much to recommend it beyond the fact that you can get out of it quite quickly. She went away to university, but returned immediately afterwards. Her two sisters have never moved away, and she still sees many people who were friends at primary school.

My life has been quite different. Since the age of 18, I have never lived within a hundred miles of Wednesfield. For quite long periods, I have been thousands of miles distant from it. Other than close relatives, I see no one that I knew as a child and when, increasingly infrequently since the death of my mother, I visit the place, I hardly recognize it, and I know no one in it. Looking back, my life does not feel like an unbroken continuum, more like a series of skins, shed as each stage closed. I did not know, as the early summer of 1958 drew towards the summer holidays, that the first of these closures was about to take place.

At some point before the end of the school year, my parents received a letter from Staffordshire Local Education Authority indicating the school to which I should go in September. It was not a celebratory letter; it did not say, "nice one! You've passed," or bureaucratic words to that effect. It merely told me that I had been allocated to "Wednesfield Grammar School." This was mystifying, for two reasons: first, it was not the Grammar School for which we had, in the jargon "expressed a preference". That was Wolverhampton Grammar School, the only school in the area with anything approaching cachet. Its buildings looked convincingly ancient; it had a fives court; and in a shrewd marketing ploy, before marketing was invented, the boys wore grey blazers. They

not appear to exist. There was no grammar school in Wednesfield.
If there had been, surely we would have noticed. My mother rang
the Civic Hall to enquire, and received the information that it was
a new, coeducational school, which had yet to be built. Until it
opened, the first 80 or so pupils would be accommodated at
Willenhall Comprehensive School.

That was a bit confusing, but the salient point was that I had
passed, the first person in my family to attend a grammar school. I
wanted to know at once whether the school would teach Latin,
because I wanted it to be as similar as possible to the Greyfriars of
the Billy Bunter stories. I had been much taken by the passages in
which Mr.Quelch frog-marches the Remove through Virgil's
Aeneid, and I longed for the day when a real-life Mr.Quelch would
utter the words,

My father assured me, on what basis I do not know, that, yes,
there would be Latin. I then reflected for a moment. I did not want
life to be all classical scholarship:

"There will be sport, wow there?"

And there would be laboratories, and homework and the cane,
and all the other features that made it clear one was moving into a
different, more grown-up, world. I barely noticed that my Dad
answered my questions in a slightly grumpy way, no doubt
recalling his own lost opportunity. We went out to a pub with a
garden that evening. I think it must have been a celebration. I
remember bowling a tennis ball across the grass at my sister,
yelling with each delivery,

"I'm a grammar-school boy."

It must have been nauseating. Normally, she would have tolerated this for no more than three seconds. She must have been under instructions to play with me. She was herself to "pass" two years later. My grandfather was at this point in the last months of his life, but must have known of my success. I hope it pleased him that I had taken the first step to getting "letters after my name."

Next day, I rushed into school, eager to see who else had "passed". Mickey and Royston hadn't: no surprise there. Gerald, like my cousin Roy, found himself condemned to the salt mines of Wardsbridge sec mod. More surprisingly, Ian found himself part of the phalanx the next phase of whose academic career would be entrusted to the care of St.George's C of E Secondary school, a hundred yards from my home, and known universally simply as "The Church." Astonishingly to me, even Arnold Hope and Gillian Wopples found themselves among the educational "goats". I was the only boy to have passed, and there was one girl, Jacqueline Meredith, whom I had seen to that point no reason to notice; nor did I change my stance. This was excellent: to be not only successful, but uniquely so. My success was drawn to public attention at assembly in front of the whole school, admittedly as part of a lament for the wholesale failure of my year, which he used as an awful warning to the younger children about what would happen to them, too, if they were idle and TOOK NO INTEREST IN WHAT THEY WERE DOING. In so doing, he of course managed to convey to most of my peers (all but two) that they were facing a future of unrelieved bleakness, rather as though their letter from the Council had allocated them to Strangeways or Wormwood Scrubs. For me, though, it was a moment of pure pleasure: this was my fifteen minutes of celebrity, and if it did not extend beyond Neachells Lane, well, my horizons were themselves not very much more extensive.

Leaving Junior School for the last time was a disconcerting experience. We did so with whoops of glee, and a gratifying feeling of being grown-up: objects of fear to smaller children. There was, though, a certain amount of bravado in this. We had all been six years at the school. Mostly, we had been bored by it, but there was a certain familiarity and security even in that tedium. Its dusty, green painted rooms, lavatorially half-tiled, had become a sort of second home, which gave us, if not challenge, excitement, magic or fascination, at least a kind of kindly acceptance, and a half-condescending warmth. We felt it was intrinsically part of a world which, though it had many imperfections, at least cared for us. We understood that we would increasingly be required to "stand on our own two feet" – Mr.Baxter was a master at choosing the right cliché for any occasion. Not all of us were too confident of our sense of balance.

By now, a week or two after the results were out, I was beginning to worry about the awful isolation that appeared to beckon. It was of course quite out of the question that I should make common cause with a girl, and in fact I do not recall ever exchanging words with Miss Meredith, She would not have felt offended by this. When my own sister came to the school three years later, I didn't speak to her either. My friends, however, were being scattered to the four corners of the Earth – or at least to one of three schools, none of which was more than a mile away. True, I would be able to see them after school, but what about during the school day? Even in this, I was too optimistic. I had no idea of the extent to which boys at sec.mods refused to associate with grammar-school boys. Well within the first year, most of my friends had melted away. The exception was Mickey. We remained friends till we were about 14, though I think that this reflected in part his own unpopularity, not unrelated to a somewhat confrontational personal style. To the familiar question: "Gorra match?"

He would, for example, reply

"Ar. My arse and yower face."

This did not always met with the reception such urbanity clearly merits.

I began to worry, too, about things such as school uniform and kit. There was a considerable list of requirements, my Mother's approach to which was unconvincing. She refused to go to the official school outfitter's, pronouncing it too far and too dear. This left me with a collection of items not all of which matched the stated requirements. For example, the official school blazer was maroon, with a badge. My mother bought one which was a much lighter red, almost pink, with no badge; the badge she purchased separately, with the intention of sewing it on, and this she did eventually do, after my second term. All items were meant to be name-tagged: there was of course no question of my mother doing this. Indeed, she denounced the requirement as unreasonable. I was therefore conspicuous in ways I did not wish to be.

Because we were at first located in Willenhall, suitably placed to enjoy the full bouquet of the potted meat factory, a school coach was supplied, and I went to the Wood End Roundabout to catch it. There were three or four boys and the same number of girls already there. Two of the boys were bowling a tennis ball to each other:

"Oy fatso," one called out, "what do you bowl?"

I ignored the insult, which I would normally have dealt with directly.

"Dunno, " I replied, "give us a bowl,"

I then gave the ball the fiercest twist my fingers were capable of imparting. It turned about a millimetre.

"Off-spin," he pronounced, "I think."

The first stop was at Woden Road School. What seemed like scores of children got on, all appropriately kitted out.

"Eh, " one said to me, "You're on the wrong bus, mate."

133

These kids clearly knew each other, and their accents were not quite like mine. We were only about a mile from my home, but their school served the other side of Wednesfield: the side that had private housing in quiet, tree-lined avenues. Virtually the whole of their top junior class had passed the eleven plus, and were now on their way, en bloc, to the grammar school. They piled on, heading for the rear of the coach:

"Come on, Aitch! Sit over here."

"Eff off, Brim, we're savin' that for Click."

"Bollocks! If Click can sit there, so can I."

I recognized only one of them: a boy called Fox, whose father was the superintendent at my Sunday School, which as his son Foxy attended ex-officio. I had not, so far as I remembered, ever spoken to him, since he hung around with a handsome, lazy boy called Langham, who, it transpired, had failed the exam, and been sent to Tettenhall College, which was one of those second rate independent schools set up to spare middle class children the trauma of contact with the masses. Foxy was, by repute, a master of crime. Later on, he was to be my accomplice in many a dirty trick.

It was an oddly isolated way to begin, in a school which was not ours. Willenhall Comprehensive was, I should now guess, one of Staffordshire's showplace schools: a vast, new, purpose-built com-prehensive school. It had a Headmaster, Dr.Tyack, who had the air and the self-confidence of a bishop. He took my form, when he remembered, for RE. Everything was very different. Boys, for example, were addressed by their surnames, girls by their Christian names. We did not mind this at all. It was certainly discriminatory, but we felt it discriminated in our favour. We were being treated like grown-ups, the girls as little kids. That, we felt, was only right and proper. There was Latin, and French, and science in proper laboratories, with rats in cages, fume cupbards and Bunsen burners that emitted a satisfying fountain when connected to the water taps.

And there was homework, not much of it, and it was not particularly demanding, but it was there, and had to be done. On my first day, I settled down to my Latin, and showed my books to my mother and father, who evinced no interest. From then on, I do not recall ever again doing homework at home. To a certain extent, and for a while, I was bright enough, and had a good enough memory, to get away with this. Most of what was set, I could do on the coach, and what had to be memorized I could usually regurgitate without special effort. As time went on, though, I was caught out more and more and forced to take refuge in the idler's traditional excuse:

"I forgot, Sir."

The failure of this plea ever to pass muster did not prevent its endless repetition, and led in later years to more and more severe punishment, including "the cane," which I did not much mind. It gave one a certain celebrity, and came nowhere near the pain we inflicted on each other on the sports field. It was not that it was difficult at home to do one's work, simply that it so obviously did not matter to anyone that the impetus to do it was wholly lost.

In many ways, the transition from primary school to grammar school was too much for me, given the unfortunate coincidence of my family background and the absence of a ready-made circle of friends in my new school. I do not blame anyone for this. The most cowardly and useless of all betrayals is that by one generation of its predecessor. I do not think my parents can be held responsible for the life I have had, and in any event most people would think that it has not been a life to complain about excessively. After all, I have an OBE to prove that I at least attained a certain level of mediocrity, thereby justifying my grandfather's prophecy that I would one day have "letters after my name." If my life has sometimes seemed more difficult to live than it should have done,

I do not see why I should ascribe only that to the influence of my family.

I remember my father once telling us an anecdote about a workmate of his. This man was going home in his workclothes, smelling of tar and soot, when he saw his son and several of his friends, resplendent in school uniform, approaching. The son affected not to see his father, and passed by without a greeting. My father went on to describe with relish the beating he had received upon his return home.

"And if yo ever did that, I'd bloody kill yer!"

I had no doubt that it would be so, and that in a certain sense it would be entirely deserved, yet I could not help feeling a certain sympathy for the boy in question (whom I did not know). Snobbery, I knew, was wrong, but I too was conscious of being ashamed of my parents. I was, after all, now at a school where we played rugger, and where the Black Country dialect was severely, though not explicitly, discouraged. One of my most deeply shaming moments was being ejected from the school choir in my first year, because of the impurity of my vowel sounds. Black Country vowels cannot, apparently, sustain musical pitch.

The gulf between me and my new schoolmates was, I now realize, nowhere near as wide as I then thought. My yardstick of middle-class respectability consisted of the Browns of the Just William stories, and of Billy Bunter and his classmates in the Remove at Greyfriars. There simply were not enough middle-class people in Wednesfield to populate a school, and there weren't any who were middle class in the style of the Browns, the Whartons and the Cherries. No doubt, there were a few who worked in Wednesfield, doctors, dentists and the like, but they did not live there. They had their homes on the other side of Wolverhampton, where the town starts to leak into Shropshire, and suburbia becomes a passable facsimile of real countryside, or in chi-chi villages, like Brewood.

From the viewpoint of the outside world, I would guess we were all much of a muchness. There are, though, many rungs of respectability within the working class, and we were by no means on the bottom one. My Dad had a reasonable job, we had a car, of some antiquity, and we were the first in our street ever to have a television, and the first to get the ITV when it started. It was not, however, poverty that embarrassed me, so much as an ill-defined sense, increasing with time, that our household simply did not function as well as others did. It did not of course occur to me that I saw other people's families as they pretended to be, ours as it was.

All children, I suspect, feel that they have a duty to be happy and to be well looked after, and a deep sense of shame if they fail in this responsibility. I was not consistently either, not because my parents were poor, or deliberately negligent, but because they were too wrapped up in their own concerns to notice the unhappiness of a child who made it his business not to impinge on their lives too much. Quite a lot of embarrassment resulted from simple incompetence. Throughout her life, my mother was generous with money, but hopeless at managing it. My father certainly gave her enough for the housekeeping, but by Monday, when we had to take in our dinner money, it was often spent. We would be told:

"Tell 'em I ay gorrit today. Yo can 'ave it on Thursday."

Of course, I did no such thing. I merely entered my usual plea of amnesia – and again on Tuesday, and Wednesday. Fortunately my Form master was relaxed about it, no doubt having a clear idea of what was actually happening. He would simply say,

"Forgot it, I suppose, Singleton?"

"Yessir," I would reply, or occasionally, with a hint of triumph and an expression of injured innocence, "Nosir, brought it."

"Ah, no less welcome for being unexpected."

In some quite crucial ways, increasingly so as time went on, I could not rely on my home, and certainly I never took any of my schoolmates there, once I went to grammar school. It could not be counted on to be tidy, but much worse than that, whenever my father was there, there was the possibility of some kind of outbreak.

As I moved into my teens, my father's mood seemed progressively to darken. He took no interest in our schooling, and was less and less visible. He was drinking more frequently, and more heavily. He never quite became drunk, and he never again beat me, after the one traumatic night, other than when he was instructed to do so by my mother, but he would come home late on Friday, Saturday and Sunday, his usually quietly sardonic manner transformed into an intolerably patronising sarcasm. My mother was not the woman to accept this; if assertiveness training had been invented then, she would not have required it. She was not prepared to accept criticism, however justified, of her abilities as cook or housekeeper, and she was more easily wound up than a top. Arguments were frequent, and occasionally broke into physical violence, usually at her instigation. Every word, every insult could be heard from the bedrooms, and both my sister and I spent every weekend for years waiting, heartsick, for the obligatory row to begin.

It did not occur to me at the time that rowing parents were not the sole prerogative of the working class. I therefore assumed that my schoolmates' home life resembled the perfumed and prissy idyll one was beginning to see in the television adverts. I was unhappy, but more than that, I was embarrassed and ashamed.

As my primary school friendships fell away, therefore, the division between my school life and my life out of school became more and more absolute. By the time I was 15, I had become an anxious recluse, conscious that there was something about myself that was fit only to be hidden away. I became fat and spotty, through over-indulgence in boiled sweets. I read voraciously, and largely ceased going out. I never invited any of my schoolmates home, and went to considerable lengths to avoid leaving or entering my house in their sight. For years, I would check that there was no one in the road before venturing out. I had no contact with girls outside school, and as little as possible in school, even though I had begun to be tormented by very strong sexual feelings, of which I felt a further degree of shame. Again and again, I failed to complete school assignments, even in subjects such as history where I read voraciously. I was regularly punished, though I now suspect not as regularly as, in strict justice, I might have been. Grammar school teachers in those days did not think that they should function as psychiatric social workers, but I must have been so patently unhappy that a little forbearance was exercised.

Not that I was wholly isolated, or in any obvious way a victim. I was one of a little crowd, far too eccentric and disorganized to be called a gang, of ne'erdowells who clustered around Foxy, attracted by his wit and capacity for ingenious mischief. In so far as I had a best friend at school, he was it. My mother told me, many years later, that he died young, killed in a car crash. I hope she was misinformed, as she was about much else. He was an indolent, good-humoured boy, who liked a laugh, and to provoke laughter in others. It was officially recognized that we tended to operate together, "Singleton," I remember the geography teacher saying one day, "whenever I see you, you are punching someone's head, and Fox, whenever I see you, you are encouraging Singleton to punch someone's head."

That rather summed it up. I supplied the muscle, Foxy the ingenuity and the daring. It greatly added to his attractiveness that he was oddly accident prone. For example, he spent some months developing the art, now forgotten, of spitting, or as we called it, "flobbing" out of the corner of his mouth so that he could spit at right angles to his direction of travel, the advantages of which must of course be apparent. One morning, he was demonstrating this much admired facility as we rode headlong down Ward's Bridge, only hundreds of yards from school. Unfortunately, he failed to detect the Latin master coming rapidly up on his outside. The latter, normally a gentle man, was so beside himself with rage I thought he was about to commit some unspeakable outrage with the bicycle pump he waved threateningly in our direction. It may not have helped that, while Foxy was palely contrite, I and two other confederates were helplessly laughing in the background.

"I didn't mean it Sir, " pleaded Foxy, "I didn't know you were there."

All to no avail. He was sentenced to three across the backside for this.

Not the least of his many subversive gifts was a preternatural control of his wind. He was in particular the accepted master of the "silent enemy:" the fart that emerged soundlessly upon the world, slowly spreading a deadly miasma, like the release of mustard gas in the First World War. We would sit in morning assembly on the back row, immediately in front of the masters and, even as we were belting out "To be a pilgrim" or some similarly elevating ditty, Foxy would let one of his masterpieces into the world. Exquisite was our enjoyment of the gagging noises emanating from the back row; complacent our sense of perfect security. How could we be detected? If detected, of what crime could we be accused? After all, no less a figure than the Head of Maths, as we would have delighted to point out, was himself notoriously flatulent.

Geography and, for different reasons, Latin were among the lessons I enjoyed. As a subject, geography was of course without any interest whatever. The Masai again put in a regular appearance, though we were now more taken than we had been by the naked breasts of their women. There was a good deal of colouring in of sea: not the least of the disadvantages of life on an island, and much incomprehensible fiddling with map references. The attraction was the teacher. I do not remember his real name. We called him "sarky Jack," and we looked forward to his lessons, not for their content , but for his skill in denunciation, and his gift for, as it now seems, somewhat laborious irony. I recollect his first encounter with a gentle, dreamy boy called Paul Beazely, who joined the school in the third year:

"You must be Beazely."

"Yes Sir."

"No need to apologise. You interest me strangely. You look to me to have a touch of the exotic about you Beazely, a hint of the tanned explorer, a touch of the tropics. Tell me Beazely, from what distant, sun-kissed land have you come to this favoured place.

"Smethwick, Sir."

It may be that our lives were rather deficient in excitement, but we greeted this exchange with delight.

"Sarky Jack was one of the few teachers consciously to play the part of the traditional schoolmaster, somewhere between Mr.Chips and Crocker –Harris. Another was our history teacher, Mr.Ellis, who must have been a very young man when I knew him. Certainly, I once saw him thirty-five years later, and he was still plump and pink-cheeked, with his hair flopping over his forehead, still wearing his Jesus scarf, still in sports jacket and flannels. He was of the school of history teaching that believes in the telling of stories. We had no truck in his lesson with primary sources. He would lean against the radiator and tell us about the past. Gustavus Adolphus, Frederick the Great, Bismark, Napoleon: all were brought to life, in their unspeakable foreignness. He had the historian's trick of always speaking in the present tense, as though observing the events he describes.

"And what does Frederick do, to celebrate the accession of his fellow monarch, the young and vulnerable Maria Theresa? He invades her territory, that's what he does!"

Mr.Ellis was not, you felt, a Tolstoyan. For him, history consisted entirely of the play of character and the clash of monstrous wills.

His colleague in the history department was quite different. Mr.Ellis had been to a Welsh college, but it had not been from choice; he had failed to get in elsewhere (this was another of his virtues; a question about his time at Oxford would invariably set him reminiscing: valuable minutes during which rehearsal for a planned test could be undertaken). His colleague, Mr Lloyd, was as Welsh as it is possible to be. I think he may indeed have been Welsh-speaking, not as common then as it is now; if so, he did not inflict it on us. His degree was from, I think, Aberystwyth . He was in every way the opposite of Mr.Ellis. Where Ellis was genial, he was severe; where Ellis chatted, he dictated notes; where Ellis was short and fat, he was immensely tall and thin; where Ellis was fair-haired, he was dark, with hair severely disciplined en brosse, with spikes sharp enough to impale a homing pigeon. He walked immensely fast, where Ellis ambled, with great swings of the leg, and no bending at the knee, each stride bringing his size thirteens crashing with a force that seemed likely to break through the mantle of the Earth. You could hear him coming miles away along the school corridors. We called him "creeping George." He was both a figure of some comedy – as a Welshman, how could he not be? – and a little terrifying. His lessons were regimented – history, for Mr.Lloyd was too serious a matter to be a fit subject for mere discussion; it consisted of facts, which had to be learnt – but somehow not quite boring. Enough narrative broke through the notetaking to remind us that there was in the end a story buried somewhere there.

I did history at A-level, alongside one other student. Mr. Lloyd taught us British History 1870-1939 and Mr.Ellis European History 1648-1870. Quite why it was decided that the "periods" should not overlap, I do not know nor why our knowledge of British – or was it English? – history should have been confined to so few decades. Our two masters maintained in the sixth form precisely the same pedagogical approach that had served them so

142

well earlier on, with the exception that Mr.Lloyd photocopied his notes and read them through to us, and we then learned them. I do not remember that the key word "discuss" featured at all prominently in Mr.Lloyd's vocabulary: that word which has saved so many generations of history examiners the intellectual effort of framing precisely the question they wish to ask:

"Frederick the Great was a bad German, but a good Prussian. Discuss."

The response to this was of course to write down all one knew about that distinguished but ambiguous monarch, in the knowledge that the examiners would reward any relevant point inadvertently mentioned. Mr.Ellis was especially fond of the word "discuss". It brought back for him the world of the Oxford tutorial. I think he would have served us sherry, had it not been frowned upon.

I remember them both with some affection, as is also true of the Latin teacher, Mr.Dacre: a Yorkshireman, but also an Oxonian: sometime scholar of Merton. He was an ascetic looking man, lean and much given to immensely long bike rides. His subject was not immediately rewarding. We had two text books. One was "Mentor", which was forbiddingly grammatical, with lists of sentences for translation from and into Latin, interspersed with explanations of morphological or syntactical points for digestion – these rendered less comprehensible by the author's unwillingness to enunciate any "rule" without immediately listing all the exceptions to it. "Civis Romanus" was by comparison light relief. It consisted of stories from Roman myth, history and legend, in Latin and intended to be morally improving, both in content and by dint of the mortification entailed in the act of translation. There were Romulus and Remus, Horatius at the Bridge, Regulus and Cincinnatus; we learned to admire the wisdom of the geese that guarded the Capitol, and to agree with Cato the Censor on the desirability of obliterating Carthage. We happily, or at least patiently, translated sentences such as:

"Do not go down to the woods, O boys! There are many wolves there."

Without questioning their lack of obvious relevance to our lives. We knew, after all, that what we were receiving was an education, the function of which was to prepare us, not for the lives we had had up to that point, but for those to which our elders and betters thought it right for us to aspire. And so, we were taught a dead language, by a "Greats" man, and were perhaps somewhat dimly aware that this was a kind of initiation into the world of Greyfriars and out of the Black Country.

Not that Mr.Dacre was an elitist figure in himself. He had retained – God knows at what cost – his Yorkshire accent, and he had about him the air of genteel poverty typical of a young schoolmaster with a wife and young children. He had a clear dedication, which in those days passed for left wing, to the ideal of sharing with working class children the advantages he had himself, somewhat adventitiously, enjoyed. He was not by any means a gifted teacher of younger children: he had no knack, for example, of devising games to make the learning of declensions or conjugations palatable. He accepted, as people did then, that learning Latin was above all an exercise in deferred gratification, and that most people could safely be relied upon to give it up well in advance of actually experiencing the gratification that was deferred.

His real passion was for poetry, which became apparent only in the sixth form. He wrote comic verse himself, of publishable quality, and was as well read in the poetry of "The Movement" as he was in Virgil, Ovid and Catullus. In sixth form Latin lessons, we would complete our stint of the Aeneid or Livy, then talk about "The Four Quartets". It was my first experience of a teacher who was not simply imparting something to me, but encouraging me to reflect, with discipline, on my own experience of literature. I gather that Mr.Dacre resigned in principle from the school when it ceased to be a grammar school. I hope he found a congenial berth, and a few like-minded souls.

These were the teachers I remember most vividly, but there were others I now recall, for wholly different reasons. My secondary education differed from primary school in many ways, but not least in that some of the teachers were not merely female, but young and beautiful, which was in those far-off times against the rules for primary teachers. Miss Cogbill, who taught us maths was tall, dark-haired and slender, and wore filmy dresses; Mrs Bradshaw was also dark, but small and curvy, with a tendency to wear tailored suits that marvellously accentuated the already generous curve of her buttocks. Mrs Bradshaw's arse has not had the literary celebration it deserves; it is worth at least a sonnet. And there was Miss Jones, pale and pre-Raphaelite, who taught us French literature, and disappointed us by becoming engaged and leaving to be married.

The Headmaster took us for mathematics, when not busily engaged with more important tasks. My sister tells me that he died only recently, in which case he must have been almost a hundred years old. As he frequently told us, he had been an athlete. He took part, in fact, in the Berlin Olympics in 1936, as a long-jumper – possibly a rather unrewarding event, since he was up against the great Jesse Owens. Whenever it was raining hard on Games afternoon, we were shown the Leni Riefenstahl film of the Olympics, with total disregard of the undesirability of exposing us to Nazi propaganda. We, of course, took no notice. The Head was, briefly and unrecognizably, said to be visible in one shot. I was never convinced. He was a pleasant, portly little man, who by the time he came to us had visibly lost any impetus he may once have had. His lessons were dull, but brief, as he invariably arrived late. You could see into his room from an upstairs corridor, and we posted lookouts to alert us to the moment of his departure. One day, they observed him tossing a ping-pong ball against the walls of his study, then diving picturesquely to catch the rebound. A little later, he arrived, as always, bustling importantly:

"Sorry to be late. I had an important telephone call."

145

God, how we laughed! And as our laughter swelled, so did his evident fury, till he seemed about to explode.

I think he cannot have been a particularly good mathematician. Certainly, he was quite unable to explain anything mathematical to me in ways that enable me to detect any rational processes of thought in the subject. It was taught as a language, with rules which you learned, but could not expect to understand; and there was no content to it. No story. Once at Parents' Evening (I think the only one my mother ever attended), he said to my mother:

"David is very clever. Only occasionally do you get boys like him, whom you can talk to on your own level."

I do not think I received this as especially complimentary.

He too was a Yorkshireman, from Leeds. I became convinced that all teachers were recruited, either from across the Pennines or from the other side of Offa's Dyke, and that this went some way to explaining their lack of resemblance to other human beings. Our form-master, Mr. Thompson, was also a Yorkshireman. He had the compensating advantages of being six feet two inches, and an extremely good cricketer. Not even these virtues, however, could make him interesting. He took us for both English and French, and invested both languages with the air of dried up antiquity that might have been expected to be characteristic of Latin. He was of the grammatical persuasion, rather than the literary, and was above all convinced that communication was the least of priorities when it came to learning languages. I never considered reading English at university, and I have always regarded France and all things French through the awful tedious prism of those long ago, dust-filled classrooms, where the settling of motes in the light of the sun was often the liveliest activity to be seen.

My grammar school education did not rate enjoyment high among the educational virtues. Each year, at speech day, we listened to the chair of governors, a Mr. Guest, who was a coal merchant in a large way of business. Each year, he droned on about service, about being a small cog in a big wheel, remembering that the team was bigger than any individual, and so on. The gist of his message was that the purpose of education was to cramp the soul: to restrict ambition to the relatively easily attainable, to shun individuality, and regard creativity with the gravest suspicion. This, after all, was what had made Britain what she was!

We of course kicked against this, by seeking opportunities for anarchy, at which Foxy was rather expert. In Chemistry, over which Mr.Shannon presided with kindly ineffectuality, we caused explosions whenever possible. In biology, we poured fluoroscene into the tadpole tank:

"Christ, they've turned my bloody tadpoles green,"cried the biology master, excitable and, inevitably Welsh. Another Welshman and victim was "Vic" Davis, who took the few of us who had opted in the third form to do German. He was a genial man: large, shambling and rather innocent. He wore the schoolmaster's uniform of a thick, tweed jacket. Presumably these were handed out as a kind of demob outfit when people completed their national service. He had a habit of wandering between the desks as we confronted the intricacies of German morphology. Knowing this, we kept our fountain pens loaded with ink, and as he wandered fired a salvo down his back. I do not know whether his colleagues or his wife ever pointed this out to him, but we did it with impunity until we became bored with the lack of reaction. It became more entertaining to attract the attention of the boy in front. When he turned round, he would receive a trail of ink, stretching from ear to ear. The girls, who of course sat on the other side of the room expressed their views on this behaviour with characteristically female lack of humour. Their views were of no interest to us, though they began as time went on to attract another kind of interest, expressed in my case by a shyness so crippling that I was for years unable to speak in the presence of a girl.

Our education was designed to elevate us from our humble backgrounds to a higher sphere: not quite that of leadership perhaps, but one at least of the significant functionary. We were, we had always to remember, small cogs in a big wheel, but not the smallest, and we were regularly reminded that from those to whom much has been given, much is expected. What the "much" was that we were given, was never wholly clear.

Our School's choice of sport (for boys, naturally; girls' sport did not matter much in those days) was designed to differentiate us from the lumpen masses that inhabited, troll-like, the surrounding secondary modern schools. They all played football. Our winter game was rugby. This caused me significant grief, and was a subject of ridicule to my remaining friends from primary school. In those days, the West Midlands were a stronghold of rugby union, with Coventry perhaps the strongest club in the country. We neither knew nor cared about this. For us – all of us – the natural rhythm of the seasons dictated that football followed cricket as surely as the first frosts followed the flight of the swallows. I still recall the shocked disbelief with which we gathered, surrounding our PE teacher, on too large and too grassy a field, with posts at either end in the shape of a gigantic H. We were allocated to positions, none of which meant anything to us, on the basis of our shape and size. Because I was large and, by then, bulky, I was told that my destiny was to be a forward. I perked up at this: being a forward to me meant opportunities to score, to achieve glory. I was swiftly to learn that the respective functions of backs and forwards in rugby are almost directly the converse of what they are in football. The backs get to pass, to run, to score. The forwards are the equivalent of the Greek phalanx. Mostly, they push, except for rare moments when the other phalanx falls apart, and there is a brief and enjoyable period of trampling upon the bodies of the fallen. Worse still, I was allocated to the second row, which I soon gathered had three functions. One was to "scrum it". This meant shoving hard in the midst of a heaving pack of sweating, farting bodies, with one's hand clasped around the buttocks of the boy in front, while a pervert explored one's intimate parts from behind. Second, there was the line-out. This entailed leaping into the air, flapping one's hands to avoid contact with the ball thrown in one's direction; it was virtually impossible to avoid injury. At best, some oaf would descend, studs protruding, onto your foot. At worst, if you were unfortunate enough to catch the ball, a fiasco appropriately described as "a maul" would form around you. Then, for some minutes, the remaining fifteen members of both packs would vie in their eagerness to dismember the unfortunate and unwilling "ball-carrier," namely you. Often, the maul would collapse and transform itself into a ruck. The wretch who was at the bottom of this would find himself vigorously stamped upon by all others. Lastly, there was "corner-flagging," which merely required you to rise from the scrum and, if the opposition had the ball, scuttle back towards your own goal line, looking intent on mayhem, but in fact hoping to time your run so as to obviate the possibility of having to engage in a tackle. This was occasionally required of all fifteen players. It seemed to me that much the most economical and practical method of stopping, while also injuring, your opponent was to smack him hard in the face as he dashed past. Next to that came the expedient of grabbing his shirt, using his own inertia to swing him round in a circle, while searching for the deepest puddle in which to deposit him. Neither course of action was allowed. The games master would yell:

"Go low, Singleton, low, low, low,"

If in an especially vindictive mood, he would stop the game and condemn one to demonstrate the correct technique, which involved obstructing a flying knee with one's unprotected face. Occasionally, too, he would penalize insufficiently manly behaviour by a sentence of "falling on the ball." This meant just what it says, with the added attraction that one's body then became an obstacle which the opposition could legitimately "ruck," i.e subject to a degree of physical abuse illegal in most other contexts.

I have come, now that I no longer have to play it, to realize that there are moments of rare excitement and precious beauty, albeit very occasional ones, in rugby. At the time, I found it hard to understand why anyone would wish to subject themselves to an activity so painful and, if you were a forward, so destitute of opportunities to shine. We played mainly on fields that resembled Flanders in 1917; I imagine this was intentional. I found it all too easy to believe that rugby had been invented by a public school man, cheating at football.

It was in those days, of course, still widely believed that the regular experience of pain, violently inflicted, was good for growing boys, particularly when set in the context of the subordination of the individual to some collective ethic, fatuously called "team spirit." Cricket was good for inflicting pain, as well, of course, though there was much more to enjoy. We did not of course play tennis; the girls did that, wielding their rackets like lettuce leaves. There was no educative value in sports which did not entail a fair risk of injury. Occasionally, when it was so wet that rugby would have entailed significant risk of drowning, we went on cross-country runs. These were popular, since it was possible to cheat by taking a short-cut and hole up for a quick fag. There was a spot where the course crossed a stream; several of us would wait there and throw more zealous competitors into the black and evil-smelling water.

I wonder how much of this our parents would have approved of, had they known of it. Of course, they did not know of it. I very much doubt whether either of my parents had any clear idea of what was on the curriculum of the grammar school. They received an annual report, on which the teachers wrote epigrams alongside boxes that read alpha double-minus stroke beta double plus (question mark). What they made of this information, no one asked them. They were invited each year to a parents' evening, and I believe mother went, after my sister joined the school. She, incidentally, was an academic star, until hitting a steep decline from the age of fifteen onwards. My father retreated ever further into his world of work, fiddling with engines, dominoes and drink. I rarely spoke to him; when I did, his conversation was largely monosyllabic.

At school, I was problematic. Nowadays, I would be excluded, or referred to some bearded drop-out in corduroy trousers for "counselling." I was morose, frequently absent, and heavily involved in subversive activity, such as assisting in the cramming of a raw potato into the exhaust of the head's Bentley. We were never, fortunately, apprehended in this, since it did a very great deal of damage. I did little or no homework, but did better in examinations than I should have done, owing to the good fortune of having an excellent memory. Alas, you cannot remember what your never learned in the first place; so my frequent absences caused me some difficulty there too. All of my absences from school were condoned by my mother, and it is some tribute to her idleness that even the prospect of my moping about the house all day did not impel her to make the minimal effort required to send me on my way.

I was not, then, a good advertisement for a grammar school education. I certainly cannot say that I enjoyed my school, and I departed from it with such little ceremony that I do not even remember the day of my leaving. All of my goodbyes have been like that: said in absentia; I have never been able to feel a degree of belonging to an institution that would persuade me to attend the leaving of it with either regret or celebration. I have made no leaving speeches, and left no circular emails to leave people wondering, "who the hell was he?"

And yet, my grammar school education served its purpose. I gained something of a grounding in one or two things that have been important in my life, despite missing out on many more that I guess would have been in the end equally valuable. I dropped science, out of boredom, and maths out of incapacity as soon as I could, for example. I did far too little music, and not enough art. But my schooling nevertheless succeeded in its fundamental purpose, which was to sever me from my childhood. This it did as completely as the machinations of the wicked Mrs.Coulter severed the children from their daimons in the Philip Pullman story. By the time I left the grammar school at 17, with rather modest qualifications, I had been changed by more than adolescence. I no longer saw the friends of my early childhood; by then, all of them were working, and happily fornicating their way towards involuntary marriages and the responsibilities of fatherhood, which were not as readily escaped in those days as they are now. I knew that I was different from them, and from my parents, and I never took the trouble to re-establish a common language. I just moved on, to what I knew would be a different destiny, far from the country in which I was born.

And when I moved on from Grammar school, it was to university, and out of the world in which I had lived until then. Out of the Black Country, out of my family, out of the class into which I had been born. When I left for university, my father and sister accompanied me to Wolverhampton High Level Station. As the train pulled out, I watched my father standing on the platform: he looked, for the first time, small, grey and old. He would live another fifteen years, and there were many times in those years that I dreamed of recovering the closeness to him I had felt, or imagined myself to have felt, as a small child. I never did.

Losing Home

I have a different scent about me now,
A different scent, and another sound:
Not the tang I had, and not the smell
Of smoky air and the faint, far-off stink
Of tar. I have wandered, and been
Half-reborn, not quite myself, not quite
Another. I can scan an Alexandrine
And follow Pindar's tortuous line,
Or test the arguments of Aristotle.
These things I know and do not possess.
They cling to me like burrs on the hide
Of a crouching animal. I live where I live
And have no home, except in recollection,
Except in far-0ff years, when I was just
A ragged arsed and roistering boy.

Biographical Note

David Singleton OBE is a poet and essayist. He lives on the outskirts of Bolton, where he spends most of his time walking on the West Pennines. He was formerly an inspector of schools and a director of a worldwide education company. He has worked in Central Europe, the Middle East and China.

Lightning Source UK Ltd.
Milton Keynes UK
UKHW010630031120
372707UK00001B/20